CONTEMPORARY

LOOK AT THE U·S·

Teacher's Guide–Literacy Level

SALLY WIGGINTON
ESL/Methods Instructor
Supervisor of Student Teaching
Urban Education Program
Associated Colleges of the Midwest
Chicago, Illinois

Project Editor
Kathy Osmus

CONTEMPORARY BOOKS

a division of NTC/CONTEMPORARY PUBLISHING COMPANY
Lincolnwood, Illinois USA

ISBN: 0-8092-4328-8

Published by Contemporary Books,
a division of NTC/Contemporary Publishing Company,
4255 West Touhy Avenue,
Lincolnwood (Chicago), Illinois 60646-1975 U.S.A.

Editorial Director Caren Van Slyke	*Illustrators* Rosemary Morrissey-Herzberg Guy Wolek
Editorial Julie Landau Craig Bolt Lisa Dillman Pat Murray	*Photo Researcher* Julie Laffin
	Art & Production Princess Louise El Jan Geist
Editorial/Production Manager Patricia Reid	
	Typography T. Alan Stone
Cover Design Lois Koehler	
	Cover photo © The Image Bank Photographer: Janeart, Ltd.

Contents

Overview

The *Look at the U.S.* series was specifically designed to help ESL teachers bring civics concepts into the classroom. This multi-level series introduces the fundamentals of U.S. history and government and is based on the federal citizenship textbooks.

This flexible series can be used in:

- special ESL/civics classes for amnesty students

- citizenship classes

- standard ESL classes

A MULTI-LEVEL SERIES

There are three books in this series so that civics concepts can be taught at the appropriate level of English proficiency.

The Literacy Level text is pictorially based with minimal text. Short passages can be read to the students. The activity-oriented exercises build students' listening and speaking skills. While some of the most basic concepts in U.S. history and government are covered, the number of new ideas is limited so the students are not overwhelmed.

Book 1 and Book 2 of this series are aimed at students who are at higher levels of English proficiency. Both books feature discussion questions that precede short passages. Each passage is followed by comprehension, vocabulary, and short writing activities. Book 2 is more challenging than Book 1 in word choice, exercise format, and the length of its sentences.

In addition to this Teacher's Guide for the Literacy Level text, there is also a Teacher's Guide for Books 1 and 2. That guide provides chapter-by-chapter ideas for supplementary activities and handouts to use in the classroom.

Throughout your work with this series, you will be given the opportunity to link important issues in American government and history to concerns facing your students in their daily lives.

You may use the order form at the back of this guide to obtain any of the other books in this series.

INSTRUCTIONAL DESIGN

The Literacy Level text is divided into three sections: America and Its People, American History Through Holidays, and American Government.

The book consists of twenty chapters. Each chapter has two components:

- The left-hand page is specifically designed for students who cannot read English. The material can be read by the teacher, and student responses are intended to be either oral or activity-based (circling, matching, etc.).

- While slightly more advanced students can use the left side of each lesson, they can also tackle the right-hand pages. These pages consist of short passages that are followed by easy comprehension or application activities. If students cannot read the passages, the teacher can read them and guide the students through the activities.

For a more in-depth look at the instructional design of the chapters, see pages 6–7 of this guide.

TEACHER'S GUIDE FOR LITERACY LEVEL TEXT

This Teacher's Guide is designed to be used with the Literacy Level text in the *Look at the U.S.* series. This guide provides:

- a rationale for this approach to introducing civics concepts to literacy and beginning level ESL students

- a lesson plan for each chapter, including a purpose for each lesson and ideas for preparing and presenting the lesson

- dozens of follow-up extension activities that provide either a life skills focus or a reinforcement of listening and speaking skills

Rationale

As a result of the Immigration Reform and Control Act of 1986 (IRCA), a need has arisen for basic instruction in U.S. history and government in ESL classes. The demand is especially great for materials for students at the literacy level. In response to this, Contemporary Books has developed *Look at the U.S.—Literacy Level* and this Teacher's Guide. While the immediate need for this book has arisen out of IRCA, the usefulness of the material far exceeds compliance with the IRCA civics requirement. The materials cover basic information that many ESL students want to know about their new country.

THE STUDENTS

As a result of IRCA, a new group of students has enrolled in ESL/civics classes. Many of these students have never attended ESL classes before. Those who have been in ESL are now faced with learning civics in addition to developing English proficiency. At this time, there are few materials available that fulfill the needs of these students and their teachers.

Look at the U.S.—Literacy Level is designed to meet the special needs of students at the literacy level. These students have a wide range of abilities. There are those who are illiterate, not only in English but also in their own language. Others are illiterate only in English or are beginning English speakers and readers. The text is designed for all of these groups, especially since students at all of these levels are often found in the same classroom.

Although the students may have varying skills, they will all have shared goals and interests. They are working toward establishing themselves in a new country, either as permanent residents or naturalized citizens. They are highly motivated to learn about the history and government of the United States.

THE CHALLENGE TO TEACHERS

The challenge for ESL teachers is to help their students learn not only English but also basic civics. Teachers will need to offer methods of instruction that are applicable for students' varying needs and skills. *Look at the U.S.—Literacy Level* and the *Teacher's Guide— Literacy Level* give teachers a wide array of tools to choose from. This approach is visual, activity-oriented, and student-centered.

Look at the U.S.—Literacy Level can be used in conjunction with a core language acquisition text. The civics text will help teachers reinforce the development of language skills through content. At the same time, students will learn a great deal about their new country. Additionally, they will acquire many higher level skills that go beyond the scope of the basic ESL text, such as the ability to read maps, timelines, and charts.

OUR APPROACH

Instructional Design

Look at the U.S.—Literacy Level is unique in its instructional design. The left-hand and right-hand pages may be used together or independently of each other.

The left-hand page of each chapter can be used by students who cannot read any English. Its purpose is to provide a starting point for learning about U.S. history and government. The emphasis is on visuals and teacher-directed activities. The printed matter on these pages serves as a listening text only—although picture cues can be used to teach certain sight words. The student-centered activities are designed to actively engage the students in using their English and applying their personal backgrounds to their new experiences in the U.S.

The right-hand page of each chapter involves more text and more extensive activities for students who can read some English and understand more advanced concepts. While the passages have been developed primarily as listening texts, students who are able can be encouraged to read along. The left-hand page may also be used as a prelesson activity to introduce the general concepts and vocabulary in the lesson.

Lesson Features

The following generally characterizes the lesson design of each chapter.

Left-hand page for literacy level students:
* beginning visual

* listening passage

* looking, listening, and/or speaking exercises: matching, circling, or oral fill-in-the-blanks

* teacher's note containing helpful hints

Right-hand page for beginning level students:
* illustration of key concept

* listening or reading passage

* exercises for group or independent work

* teacher's note containing helpful hints

A Student-Centered Approach to Content

The purpose of the Literacy Level text is to introduce students with low levels of English proficiency to very basic American history and government concepts. The most effective way to do this is to make the unfamiliar concepts relevant to people's own lives. The Literacy Level text and the Teacher's Guide constantly link issues to students' own experiences and cultural backgrounds. Therefore, at the same time that the students are developing English proficiency, they are acquiring knowledge that will help them participate more actively in American society.

Organization of Student Text

Section 1: America and Its People

Students first learn personal identification information, then broaden their perspective to the local, state, national, and global levels. Personal experiences are often drawn upon to make content more easily understood.

Section 2: American History Through Holidays

Holidays are a familiar concept to students and provide a unique opportunity to introduce the history of a nation. Basic concepts can be taught in an enjoyable and personal manner that is easily understood. Additional concepts, such as cardinal and ordinal numbers and calendar skills, can also be reinforced in this context.

Section 3: American Government

In keeping with the student-centered approach, government concepts are related to exposure that students have already had to laws, courts, and the permanent residency process.

GENERAL TEACHING TIPS

This Teacher's Guide provides four components for each page of the student text.

These chapter-by-chapter notes begin on page 10. The components for each lesson are:

1. Purpose

2. Preparation

3. Presentation

4. Extension activities

The **Purpose** identifies the basic competencies and the key vocabulary presented in each lesson.

Ideas for **Preparation** introduce each lesson. As you do these activities, identify the knowledge the students are bringing to each particular lesson, and reinforce and expand upon that knowledge. This involves an oral introduction to the material. It may also involve discussion among the students. Key vocabulary should also be initially presented.

During **Presentation**, the use of visuals often helps literacy level students understand and retain key concepts and vocabulary. Additionally, vocabulary words can be taught in the context of a sentence or through the use of objects or pictures.

The presentation of the materials will be most successful if the following steps are taken:

1. When you read aloud, read slowly. Do not distort the language, but make sure you enunciate the words clearly.

2. Read each sentence or passage at least twice.

3. Stop and ask clarifying questions to check students' comprehension.

4. You need to make your own decision on how to use the exercises, based on the students' speaking, reading, and writing abilities. All of the exercises in the book can be used as oral, writing, or reading practice.

5. When an exercise requires the students to perform a specific task, such as matching, be sure to show the students what is required of them before they begin the exercise.

Extension Activities provide opportunities to expand on the four language skills of listening, speaking, reading, and writing. These exercises also function as reviews or as application of the students' new knowledge. Extension Activities often allow the students to reflect on and share personal experiences and viewpoints.

Extension Activities begin on page 50.

SUMMARY

Introducing history and government concepts to low-level students is a unique challenge for ESL teachers. At the same time, there are new opportunities to enrich students' knowledge about their new country and perspectives about their own personal and cultural backgrounds. We hope that *Look at the U.S.* will afford you an easy and enjoyable way to accomplish these goals.

Sample Chapter

The following sample chapter from *Look at the U.S.—Literacy Level* describes specific features and their respective purposes. The pages of each lesson may be used independently or interdependently.

Please note that Extension Activities are provided at the back of this Teacher's Guide to further involve students in the learning process.

The appropriate holiday indicated on a calendar

Brief and explicit directions

Visual(s) to promote discussion and provide a prelistening activity

Brief listening passage containing a limited number of key concepts and discussion questions

Activity-based exercise reflecting the content of the listening passage and introducing pictures with corresponding sight words

Suggestions to aid in your presentation

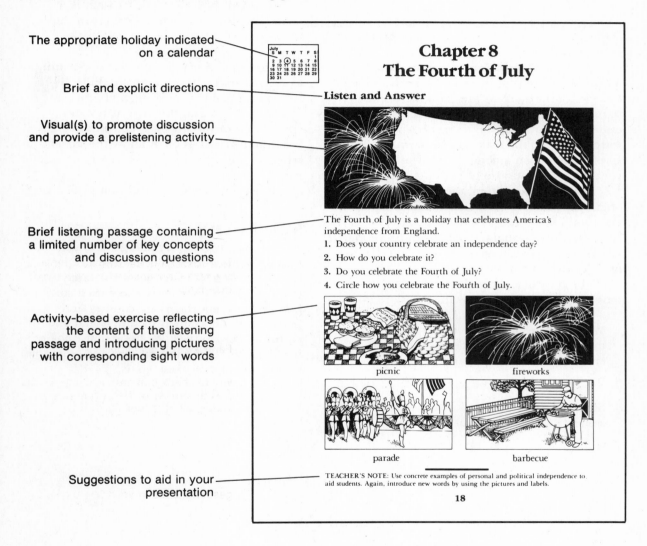

Chapter 8
The Fourth of July

Listen and Answer

The Fourth of July is a holiday that celebrates America's independence from England.

1. Does your country celebrate an independence day?
2. How do you celebrate it?
3. Do you celebrate the Fourth of July?
4. Circle how you celebrate the Fourth of July.

picnic

fireworks

parade

barbecue

TEACHER'S NOTE: Use concrete examples of personal and political independence to aid students. Again, introduce new words by using the pictures and labels.

18

The left-hand page is designed to provide basic content instruction for students who are not literate in English.

Visual(s) to reinforce content and aid comprehension

Learn About American Independence

The Fourth of July is an important holiday in the U.S. We call this holiday Independence Day to celebrate our freedom.

In 1776, England had 13 colonies in America. The American colonies were not free. The colonists wrote the Declaration of Independence to tell England that they wanted to be free.

The colonies fought a war against England. This war was called the American Revolution. The colonies won and became the United States of America in 1783.

Content passage to be used as listening or reading text. Contains key concepts with minimal detail

✔ Check Yes or No

Brief and explicit directions

1. The American Revolution was fought against Spain.   Yes ☐ No ☐

2. We celebrate the Fourth of July to remember U.S. independence.   Yes ☐ No ☐

3. My native country celebrates an independence day.   Yes ☐ No ☐

Activity to check comprehension—may be used as an oral or written exercise, depending on students' abilities

TEACHER'S NOTE: Before beginning the reading, explain that the picture shows soldiers fighting in the American Revolution.

19

Suggestions to aid in your presentation

The right-hand page is designed for low-beginning level students who can handle more complicated concepts.

Teacher's Guide Notes

The following chapter-by-chapter notes provide suggestions for presenting each lesson. You will note that there are specific guidelines for both the left-hand page of each chapter (for literacy level students) and the right-hand page of each chapter (for beginning level students). Each set of chapter notes contains the following:

- lesson objectives
- prelesson suggestions and activities to orient the students to vocabulary and new concepts
- step-by-step guidelines for presenting the lesson

Also included are page references for Extension Activities that build comprehension or develop a life-skills focus for the materials. Both lessons and Extension Activities can be adapted to fill your and your students' needs.

PURPOSE

1. To answer personal identification questions and to ask basic questions about other people.

2. To read the numbers in an address.

3. To learn key vocabulary: *name*, *address*, *city*, and *state*.

PREPARATION

1. Before opening the book, talk about yourself to introduce the basic vocabulary.

   "My name is
   _____ .

   "My address is
   _____ .

   "I live in _____ ,
                    (city)
   _____ ."
      (state)

2. Demonstrate how to read numbers in addresses. Begin with the example of your own address. Then write different possible address numbers on the board, and have the students practice reading the numbers.

3. Write the key vocabulary on the board. Define each word by illustration or example. Have the students repeat each word.

PRESENTATION

Listen and Repeat

1. Have the students open their books to page 2. Then have them look at and discuss what they see in each picture.

2. After discussing the pictures, read the sentences about Monica to the class. Explain that the *W.* in *W. Monroe* means *west*.

3. Read the sentences a few more times. Then ask the students to repeat the sentences after you, one sentence at a time.

4. Write the sentences on the board. Read each sentence aloud while tracking the words with your finger.

5. Then ask comprehension questions about Monica: *"What is her first name? What is her last name? What is her address? What city does she live in? What state does she live in?"*

Chapter 1
My Story

Listen and Repeat

My name is Monica Gonzales.

My address is 127 W. Monroe Street.

I live in Chicago, Illinois.

Listen and Answer

1. What is your name? My name is _____ .
2. What is your address? My address is _____ .
3. Where do you live? I live in _____ , _____
                                          (city)   *(state)*

TEACHER'S NOTE: Use the pictures to reinforce the concepts of "address," "street" (avenue, road, etc.), "city," and "state" (the focus of the next lesson). Explain the "W." in W. Monroe.

2

Listen and Answer

1. Ask the students the questions on page 2. Have them answer you.

2. Have the students repeat the questions after you read them.

3. Let the students practice asking the questions. They should begin by asking you, then continue by asking each other.

Extension Activities begin on page 50.

PURPOSE

1. To practice filling in forms.

2. To learn key vocabulary: *age, single, married, city, state, country, male, female,* and *signature*.

PREPARATION

1. Before having students open their books, talk about yourself to introduce the new vocabulary.

2. Use a wall map of the United States or the map on page 50 of the student text to point out the state in which you live.

3. Write the key vocabulary on the board. Define each word by example. Have the students repeat each word.

4. Demonstrate a signature. First print your name on the board, then put your signature in cursive writing next to it. Let the students practice printing their names, then writing in cursive. (Pages 54–55 of the student text contain practice in printing the alphabet.)

PRESENTATION

Learn About Monica

1. Have the students open their books to page 3, and direct their attention to the house number and the street sign in the picture.

2. After discussing the picture, read the paragraph about Monica. If students are able, encourage them to read the passage, either silently or out loud.

3. After the students hear the paragraph about Monica two or three times, ask them to repeat each sentence.

4. Then write the sentences about Monica on the board, and read them aloud, tracking them with your finger.

5. Ask questions about Monica, based on the paragraph: *"Where does Monica live? How old is she? Is she married or single? Is she male or female?**, etc.

Write About Monica

1. Copy the top form from page 3 onto the board. Ask the students questions about Monica, and fill in the form as they respond to the questions.

Learn About Monica

My name is Monica Gonzales.
I live in Chicago, Illinois.
My address is 127 W. Monroe Street.
I am 23 years old and married.
I am from Rodeo, Durango.
The state of Durango is in the country of Mexico.

Write About Monica

Name: _____
   (Last)   (First)
Address: _____
   (Number)   (Street)
   _____
   (City)   (State)
Sex: Male ___ Female ___   Age: ___
                          Signature: _____

Write About Yourself

Name: _____
   (Last)   (First)   (Middle)
Address: _____
   (Number)   (Street)
   _____
   (City)   (State)   (Zip Code)
Sex: Male ___ Female ___   Age: ___
                          Signature: _____

TEACHER'S NOTE: First, use information about yourself as an example. It may also be necessary to demonstrate the difference between the concepts of "name" and "signature." Explain the "W." in W. Monroe.

3

---

2. Ask the students to copy the information about Monica.

Write About Yourself

1. Based on the bottom form on page 3, ask the students questions about themselves. Have them answer orally.

2. Then write another blank form on the board. Ask one student questions about himself, and fill in the form with the appropriate information. Then help individual students to fill in the forms in their books.

Extension Activities begin on page 51.

---

*If the students have trouble with the terms male and female, see Extension Activity 3 on page 51.

PURPOSE

1. To learn the differences between city, state, and country.

2. To state the city and state of residence.

3. To learn key vocabulary: *city, state,* and *country.*

PREPARATION

1. Before having the students open their books, talk about yourself to introduce vocabulary. (Use the sentences on page 4 as a guide for vocabulary items.)

2. Use a wall map of the United States that all of the students can see. Point to the entire map, and explain that there are fifty states.

3. Now point to the state you live in. Then point to the city you live in.

4. Write the key vocabulary on the board. Define each word by illustration or example. Have the students repeat each word.

PRESENTATION

Listen and Repeat

1. Have the students open their books to page 4. Then have them look at and discuss each picture.

2. After discussing the pictures, read the sentences about Carlos to them.

3. After the students hear the sentences a few times, have them repeat the sentences, one at a time.

4. Write the sentences on the board. Then read them while tracking each word with your finger.

5. Ask the following questions about Carlos: *"What is his first name? What is his last name? What city does he live in? What state does he live in? What country does he live in?"*

6. Ask a student to come up to the wall map and point to California. Then ask the student to point to Sacramento.

7. Point to San Francisco and Los Angeles on the map, showing their relationship to Sacramento. (Students may be more familiar with San Francisco and Los Angeles as cities in California than with Sacramento.)

Chapter 2
In the U.S.

Listen and Repeat

I am Carlos Sanchez.

I live in Sacramento, California.

I live in the United States.

Listen and Answer

1. What city do you live in? I live in _____.
2. What state do you live in? I live in _____.
3. Point to your state on the map of the U.S. on page 5.
4. What country do you live in? I live in _____.

TEACHER'S NOTE: First, familiarize students with the U.S. map. Then use the pictures to illustrate the differences between "city," "state," and "country."

4

Listen and Answer

1. Ask individual students the questions on page 4. They should answer orally. Ask a student to come up to the map and point to the state he lives in. Have another student come and point to the city (or area) he lives in.

2. Have the students practice asking questions 1, 2, and 4 in unison.

3. Have the students work in pairs asking and answering the questions.

Extension Activities begin on page 52.

PURPOSE

1. To learn about the state capitals and Washington, D.C.

2. To learn basic map reading skills: north, south, east, and west.

3. To learn key vocabulary: *capital*, *leader*, and *Washington, D.C.*

PREPARATION

1. Review the words *city* and *state*.

2. Explain that each state has a capital city. Write the word *capital* on the board.

3. Explain that a capital city is the place where the leaders of the government work. Write the word *leader* on the board. Say that the leaders of the United States are the president and the vice president. Also say that the leader of a state is the governor.

4. Ask the students, *"How many states are in the United States?"*

5. Tell the students they are going to read about the states and about Washington, D.C. Washington, D.C., is the capital city of the entire United States.

PRESENTATION

Learn About the United States

1. Have the students open their books to page 5. Have them discuss the map at the top of the page and point to their state.

2. After discussing the map, read the passage to the students. If students are able, encourage them to read the passage, either silently or out loud.

3. Ask comprehension questions about the passage: *"Where do the leaders of the country work? What is the capital of the United States? How many states are in the United States?"*

Listen and Answer

1. Call on individual students to answer questions 1, 2, and 3 in the book. Point to the appropriate place on a map of the United States as they respond.

Learn About the United States

The leaders of a country work in the capital city. The capital of the whole United States is Washington, D.C.

There are 50 states in the United States. Each state in the U.S. also has a capital city.

This map shows Washington, D.C., and the 50 states.

Listen and Answer

1. What is the capital of the U.S.?
2. What state do you live in?
3. What is the capital of your state?
4. Name a state in the East.
5. Name a state in the West.
6. Is your native country divided into states?
7. What is the capital of your native country?

TEACHER'S NOTE: Use the map on this page to illustrate the concepts of "state" and the "capital" of a country. Also, explain the concept of "north," "south," "east," and "west."

5

2. Draw a compass on the board similar to the compass on the map. Use a map to demonstrate north, south, east, and west.

3. Ask basic map reading questions: *"Is Texas in the South? Is North Carolina in the West?"* Ask students to respond in complete sentences: *"Yes, Texas is in the South. No, North Carolina is not in the West."*

4. Ask questions 4 and 5 from the text.

5. Ask individual students questions 6 and 7, about their native countries.

Extension Activities begin on page 53.

PURPOSE

1. To work on basic map reading skills.

2. To say the names of the students' native cities and countries.

3. To learn key vocabulary: *large, small, near, far,* and *island.*

PREPARATION

1. Tell the students that they will be learning about different countries. Use yourself as an example: *"I am from Houston, Texas, in the United States."*

2. Ask the students the name of the cities and countries they are from. As the students respond, point to their countries on the map on pages 48-49 of the student text.

3. Write the following words on the board: *near* and *far*. Demonstrate the meaning of these words by using students or objects in the class. Reinforce this with students' countries, for example, *"Is Mexico near the U.S.?"*

4. Write the following words on the board: *small* and *large*. Demonstrate the meaning of these words by using classroom objects.

5. Tell the students that they will be reading about a woman from Haiti. Write the word *Haiti* on the board. Explain that Haiti is an island. Either define *island* or draw a picture. Ask students, *"Are you from an island?"*

PRESENTATION

Listen and Repeat

1. Have the students open their books to page 6. Then have them look at and discuss each picture.

2. Read the sentences. Have students repeat each sentence, one at a time.

3. Ask questions about Merilee and Haiti: *"What is her first name? What is her last name? What city is she from? Is Haiti a large country or a small country? Is Haiti near or far from the United States?"*

4. Ask individual students questions about themselves and their native countries: *"What city are you from? Is your city large or small? What country*

Chapter 3
In the World

Listen and Repeat

My name is Merilee LaRue.

Haiti is a small country.
Haiti is on an island near the
United States.

I am from Port-au-Prince.
Port-au-Prince is a large city in
Haiti.

Listen and Do

1. Find Haiti on the large map. Circle it.
2. Find the United States. Put an X on it.
3. Find the Atlantic Ocean. Put a □ on it.
4. Find the Gulf of Mexico. Put a △ on it.

TEACHER'S NOTE: Make sure the concepts of "city," "country," and "island" are clear. Use examples to show the differences between "large," "small," "near," and "far."

6

---

are you from? Is your native country large or small?"

5. Ask students questions, providing them with an opportunity to answer using the negative.
   Teacher: Are you from Haiti?
   Student: No, I'm not. I'm from
   _____.

Listen and Do

1. Help individual student do tasks 1-4.

2. Have the class complete the exercise in their books.

Extension Activities begin on page 53.

PURPOSE

1. To continue working on basic map reading skills.

2. To learn the concept of continents.

3. To learn key vocabulary: *continent, Africa, Antarctica, Asia, Australia, Europe, North America,* and *South America.*

PREPARATION

1. Illustrate the difference in size between a city, state, and country. Teach the phrases *smaller than* and *larger than.* Use classroom objects to aid in instruction.

2. Write *yes* and *no* on the board. Ask the students, *"Is a city smaller than a state?"* Point to the answer they give you. Ask other questions about size, for instance: *"Is a state smaller than a city? Is a continent larger than a state?"*

3. Write the key vocabulary on the board. Define each word by example. Have the students repeat each word.

4. Tell the students: *"We are going to read about continents. A continent is a large area of land. Some of the continents have many countries on them."*

PRESENTATION

Learn About the World

1. Have students open their books to page 7, then look at the map. Say the names of the continents aloud. Have the students repeat the names of the continents.

2. Read the paragraph about the continents aloud to the students several times. If students are able, encourage them to read the passage, either silently or out loud.

3. Ask comprehension questions about the reading: *"What is a continent? How many continents are there in the world? Which continent is the United States on?"*

Listen and Answer

1. Ask the students to name their native countries. Point to each country on a large world map or the map on pages 48-49 of the student text.

2. Ask each student to name the continent their native country is on.

Learn About the World

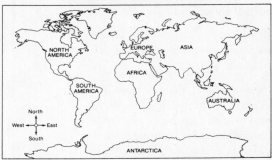

There are 7 continents in the world. A continent is a large area of land. The United States is on the continent of North America.

Listen and Answer

1. What country are you from? I am from _____.

2. What continent is your native country on? My native country is on the continent of _____.

Look at a World Map

1. Name 2 countries in North America.
2. Name 2 countries in South America.
3. Name 2 countries in Europe.
4. Name 2 countries in Africa.
5. Name 2 countries in Asia.

TEACHER'S NOTE: First, go over the continents on the map on this page. Then have students refer to the world map on pages 48 and 49 to answer the last five questions.

7

Look at a World Map

1. Point to North America on a world map. Have the students follow on the world map on pages 48-49 in their books. Have students name two countries in North America. (Remember that Mexico and Central America are in North America.) Write the two countries on the board.

2. Do the same with questions 2-5.

Extension Activities begin on page 54.

PURPOSE

1. To understand that people have been immigrating to the U.S. for a long time.

2. To answer personal questions about nationality and date of arrival in the United States.

3. To learn key vocabulary: *nationality* and *language.*

PREPARATION

1. First focus on dates. Write a year on the board and show students how it is said, for example, *19—89.*

2. Ask individual students, *"When did you come to the United States?"*

3. Review the concept of country: *"Stella is from Poland. Hua is from Vietnam."* Distinguish between the idea of country and nationality: *"Stella is from Poland. She is Polish."*

4. Write the language(s) you speak on the board. Say, *"I speak English and _____."* Ask the students, *"What languages do you speak?"* Make sure you include English for each student.

5. Tell the students that they will be reading about a man from South Korea. Write *South Korea* on the board. Point to South Korea on a world map.

6. Write the key vocabulary on the board. Define each word by example. Have the students repeat each word.

PRESENTATION

Listen and Repeat

1. Have the students open their books to page 8. Then have them discuss the picture. Ask: *"Where do you think he is from? How old do you think he is?"*

2. Read about Young Cho. Write the sentences on the board. Read the sentences again, tracking the words with your finger.

3. Ask comprehension questions about Young Cho: *"What is his first name? What is his last name? Where is he from? What nationality is he? What languages does he speak? When did he come to the U.S.?"*

4. Ask individual students questions 1-5.

5. Have the students practice asking and answering the questions.

Chapter 4
From Many Countries

Listen and Repeat

My name is Young Cho.
I am from South Korea.
I am Korean.
I speak Korean and English.
I came to the U.S. in 1976.
I came to the U.S. by airplane.

1. Where are you from? I am from _____.
2. What is your nationality? I am _____.
3. What languages do you speak? I speak _____ and English.
4. When did you come to the U.S.? I came to the U.S. in _____.
5. How did you come to the U.S.? I came to the U.S. by _____.

Show How People Came to the U.S.

Name	Airplane ✈	Boat 🚢	Bus 🚌	Foot 👣	Other ?
Young Cho	X				

TEACHER'S NOTE: Make the distinction between "country" and "nationality" by example—America-American, Vietnam-Vietnamese, etc. Be sure students understand the chart.

8

Show How People Came to the U.S.

1. Before beginning the chart exercise, familiarize students with the types of transportation. Go over the example of Young Cho.

2. Draw a copy of the chart on the board. Write a student's name in the appropriate column. Have that student tell how he came to the U.S. Put an X in the correct column. Repeat the exercise with others. Students can also ask each other and fill in the charts in their books.

Extension Activities begin on page 54.

PURPOSE

1. To continue learning the names of different countries and nationalities.

2. To learn key vocabulary: *nationality, Greek,* and *Polish.*

PREPARATION

1. Talk about your own family's immigration to the U.S. Tell the approximate year your family came to the U.S. Show on a world map where your family is from.

2. Tell the class that they are going to read about two people: a Greek man and a Polish woman. Write the two nationalities on the board: *Greek* and *Polish.* Have the students guess the name of the country each person is from. Show the students each of the countries on the world map.

3. Write the key vocabulary on the board. Define each word by illustration or example. Have the students repeat each word.

PRESENTATION

Learn About These People

1. Have the students open their books to page 9. Then have them look at and discuss each picture. Ask: *"Where do you think he/she is from? How old do you think he/she is?"*

2. After discussing each picture, read each passage two or three times. If students are able, encourage them to read the passage, either silently or out loud.

3. Ask comprehension questions about each character: *"What is his/her name? Where is he/she from? What nationality is he/she? When did he/she come to the U.S.?"*

4. Write the following sentences on the board, having the students supply the correct answers. Write them in the blanks. *He is from Greece. He is _____. She is from Poland. She is _____.*

Learn About These People

I am Bill Nikos.
I am from Greece.
I am Greek.
I speak Greek and English.
I came to the U.S. in 1908.

I am Stefania Kroll.
I am from Poland.
I am Polish.
I speak Polish and English.
I came to the U.S. in 1982.

Write About Yourself and Copy the Sentences

1. I am from _____.
   (country)

   _____

2. I am _____.
   (nationality)

   _____

3. I speak _____ and English.
   (language)

   _____

4. I came to the U.S. in _____.
   (year)

   _____

TEACHER'S NOTE: First, present your own personal information as an example. Then do this exercise orally before having students write.

9

Write About Yourself and Copy the Sentences

1. Ask each student the following questions: *"What country are you from? What nationality are you? What languages do you speak? When did you come to the U.S.?"*

2. Have the students write each answer in their books. Let them first fill in the blank, then encourage them to copy the entire sentence.

Extension Activities begin on page 54.

PURPOSE

1. To recognize and say the months of the year.
2. To recognize and say the days of the week.
3. To read a calendar.
4. To learn key vocabulary: *month, year, week,* and *day.*

PREPARATION

1. Ask the students, *"What month is it?"* Write the month on the board.
2. Show a twelve-month calendar. Say each month aloud.
3. Write the key vocabulary on the board. Define each word by illustration or example. Have the students repeat each word.

PRESENTATION

Learn the Months of the Year

1. Have the students open their books to page 12. Then have them look at the calendar at the top of the page. Say each month, and have the students repeat each month after you. Repeat this procedure as often as necessary.
2. After discussing the calendar, ask questions 1 and 2.
3. Write the twelve months on the board with the abbreviations next to them, *January—Jan.,* etc. Number the months one through twelve.
4. Write today's date three different ways: for example, *January 3, 1997; Jan. 3, 1997;* and *1/3/97.* Explain to the students that they may see dates written in any of these three ways.
5. Have the students read and say a few examples of dates written in different forms.
6. Copy question 3 onto the board. Call on individual students to match the months.
7. Help students do question 3 in their books.

Chapter 5
The Calendar

Learn the Months of the Year

1. How many months are in a year? There are ____ months in a year.
2. Repeat the names of the months. The months are ____.
3. Match the Months

Jan.	November
Feb.	September
Sept.	January
Nov.	December
Dec.	February

AUGUST

Sunday	Monday	Tuesday	Wednesday	Thursday	Friday	Saturday
		1	2	3	4	5
6	7	8	9	10	11	12

Learn the Days of the Week

1. How many days are in a week? There are ____ days in a week.
2. Name the days of the week. The days of the week are ____.

TEACHER'S NOTE: Students should be encouraged to learn the days and months in order and as sight words. Students' personal dates such as birthdays and anniversaries may also be circled on the calendar.

12

Learn the Days of the Week

1. Have the students look at the days of the week on page 12. Say each day, and have the students repeat after you. Repeat the procedure if necessary.
2. After discussing the days of the week, ask the students: *"What day is it today? How many days are in a week?"* Then have the students say the days of the week in order.

Extension Activities begin on page 55.

PURPOSE

1. To know important American historical holidays.

2. To discuss important holidays in the students' native cultures.

3. To practice finding dates on a calendar.

4. To learn key vocabulary: *holiday* and *calendar*.

PREPARATION

1. Using a wall calendar, ask individual students to come up and circle the third Monday in January, February 12, February 22, the last Monday in May, July 4, the first Monday in September, the second Monday in October, and the fourth Thursday of November. Tell them the name of each holiday as they circle the date.

2. Use the list of cardinal and ordinal numbers on page 47 in the student text to differentiate, for example, *three* and *third*. Use an ordinal number in context, for example, *"the third Monday in January."*

3. Tell the students that these dates are all important holidays in the U.S. Write the word *holiday* on the board. Define *holiday* as a day to remember a special event. Tell students that often people do not have to work on holidays.

4. Ask individual students the name and date of one important holiday in their native countries. Circle the dates on the wall calendar in a different color from the U.S. holidays.

5. Write the key vocabulary on the board. Define each word by illustration or example. Have the students repeat each word.

PRESENTATION

Learn About the Holidays

1. Have the students open their books to page 13.

2. Read about the holidays to the students. If students are able, encourage them to read the passage, either silently or out loud.

3. Ask individual students: *"In your native country, what special holidays*

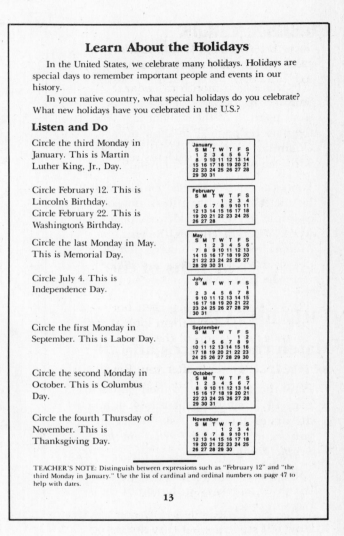

Learn About the Holidays

In the United States, we celebrate many holidays. Holidays are special days to remember important people and events in our history.

In your native country, what special holidays do you celebrate? What new holidays have you celebrated in the U.S.?

Listen and Do

Circle the third Monday in January. This is Martin Luther King, Jr., Day.

Circle February 12. This is Lincoln's Birthday.
Circle February 22. This is Washington's Birthday.

Circle the last Monday in May. This is Memorial Day.

Circle July 4. This is Independence Day.

Circle the first Monday in September. This is Labor Day.

Circle the second Monday in October. This is Columbus Day.

Circle the fourth Thursday of November. This is Thanksgiving Day.

TEACHER'S NOTE: Distinguish between expressions such as "February 12" and "the third Monday in January." Use the list of cardinal and ordinal numbers on page 47 to help with dates.

13

do you celebrate? What new holidays have you celebrated in the U.S.?"

Listen and Do

1. Write the holidays on the board, saying each slowly. Explain that the students will be studying each of these holidays in the next eight chapters.

2. Have the students circle the appropriate dates on their calendars on page 13.

Extension Activities begin on page 55.

PURPOSE

1. To recognize the name *Christopher Columbus.*

2. To understand that American Indians were already living in the Americas when Columbus arrived.

3. To learn that the second Monday in October is Columbus Day.

4. To learn key vocabulary: *Columbus, Indians,* and *parade.*

PREPARATION

1. Show the month of October on a calendar. Circle the second Monday. Ask students, *"What holiday is this?"*

2. Summarize the story of Columbus from page 15 of the student text. Use the map on page 15 to show how Columbus "ran into" North America while he was looking for Asia.

3. Write the key vocabulary on the board. Define each word by illustration or example. Have the students repeat each word. When discussing the term *Indians,* explain to students that these people are native Americans. They were the first people in America.

PRESENTATION

Match the Pictures and the Sentences

1. Have the students open their books to page 14. Then have them look at and discuss each picture. Ask: *"What do you see in the picture? What are the people doing?"*

2. After discussing the pictures, go over the three sentences at the top of the page in order.

3. Now tell students that they are going to match each sentence with a picture.

4. Reread sentence 1. Ask students to point to the picture that shows American Indians. Have them write the number 1 in the line below that picture. Continue with sentences 2 and 3.

Chapter 6
Columbus Day

Match the Pictures and the Sentences

1. American Indians were living in America.

2. Christopher Columbus landed in America in 1492.

3. On the second Monday in October, we celebrate Columbus Day with parades.

TEACHER'S NOTE: First, read or summarize the story of Columbus on page 15 and answer students' questions. Then read the sentences above, one at a time. Have students write the number of the sentence beneath the corresponding picture.

14

Extension Activities begin on page 55.

PURPOSE

1. To learn historical information about Christopher Columbus.

2. To practice basic map reading skills.

3. To learn key vocabulary: *explorer, money, boats, queen, sail,* and *Indians.*

PREPARATION

1. Show the month of October on a calendar. Circle the second Monday. Ask students, *"What holiday is this?"*

2. Write the names of the locations important to the Columbus story on the board: *Italy, Spain, India,* and *America.* Point to each location on the map. Write the name of the corresponding nationalities: *Italy—Italian, Spain—Spanish, India—Indian, America—American* or *American Indian (Native American).*

3. Have the students practice the following sentences orally: *"He is from Italy. He is Italian. She is from Spain. She is Spanish. He is from India. He is Indian. She is from America. She is American."*

4. Write the key vocabulary on the board. Define each word by illustration or example. Have the students repeat each word.

5. Have the students look at the pictures of Columbus and American Indians on page 14. Ask students what they think is happening in each picture.

PRESENTATION

Learn About Christopher Columbus

1. Have the students open their books to page 15. Then have them look at and discuss the map at the top of the page. Point out the continents, countries, and the three boats.

2. Read each statement about Columbus. Pause after each, and help students perform the accompanying activity. Walk around to make sure students are doing the activity correctly. Encourage students to help each other.

**Learn About
Christopher Columbus**

Christopher Columbus was an Italian explorer.

Put an X on Italy.

He wanted to go to India.

Put a ✓ on India.

He got money and boats from the Queen of Spain.

Put a △ on Spain.

Columbus and his men sailed in 3 boats.

Circle the 3 boats.

In 1492, Columbus landed in North America. He thought he was in India.

Put a □ on North America.

There were people already living on the land. Columbus called the people Indians.

Draw a line from Spain to North America.

TEACHER'S NOTE: After the story and activity are combined, the story may be read in its entirety by covering the right-hand column.

15

---

3. Cover the right side of the page. Read the sentences about Columbus. If students are able, encourage them to read the passage, either silently or out loud.

4. Ask comprehension questions: *"Who was Columbus? Where did he want to go? How did he come to America? What happened in 1492? Why did Columbus call the people who lived on the land Indians?"*

Extension Activities begin on page 56.

PURPOSE

1. To learn why Thanksgiving is celebrated.

2. To talk about how Thanksgiving is celebrated today.

3. To discuss students' own stories about their arrivals to the U.S.

4. To learn key vocabulary: *winter, spring, summer, fall, house, apartment, church,* and *Thanksgiving.*

PREPARATION

1. Ask the students, *"Do you remember when Columbus came to America?"*

2. Write *1492* ———➤ *1620* on the board. Explain that between 1492 and 1620 many more explorers came from Europe to the new land called America.

3. Show the month of November on a calendar. Circle the fourth Thursday. Ask students, *"What holiday is this?"*

4. Summarize the history of Thanksgiving from page 17 of the student text. Use the pictures on that page to illustrate your talk. Tell the students this is the story of the first Thanksgiving.

5. Write the key vocabulary on the board. Define each word by illustration or example. Have the students repeat each word.

PRESENTATION

Look and Listen

1. Have the students open their books to page 16. Then have them look at the picture at the top of the page. Ask the students: *"Who is this a picture of? Workers? Friends? Family? How can you tell? What are they doing?"*

2. After discussing the picture, read the sentence underneath the picture two or three times.

3. Write on the board: *I give thanks for* _____. Ask the students what they are thankful for. Write on the board what the students tell you.

Chapter 7
Thanksgiving Day

Look and Listen

Americans celebrate Thanksgiving to give thanks for family, friends, food, and health.

Circle Your Answer

1. In what season did you come to the U.S.?

winter   spring   summer   fall

2. Where did you live when you came to the U.S.?

a house   an apartment   a church

TEACHER'S NOTE: Before doing the exercises, summarize the story about the Pilgrims on page 17 to the students. Introduce new words using the pictures and labels.

16

Circle Your Answer

1. Tell students that you will be comparing their arrival to the U.S. with that of the Pilgrims.

2. Ask the students question 1. Have them circle the appropriate picture.

3. Ask the students question 2. Have them circle the appropriate picture.

4. Ask the students to tell the year that they came to the U.S.

Extension Activities begin on page 56.

PURPOSE

1. To learn about the first Thanksgiving.

2. To discuss how Thanksgiving is celebrated today.

3. To learn key vocabulary: *celebrate, Pilgrims, England,* and *Indians.*

PREPARATION

1. Show the month of November on a calendar. Circle the fourth Thursday. Ask students, *"What holiday is this?"*

2. Use the picture on page 16 as an introduction. Ask the students: *"What are they doing in the picture? Have you ever been to a Thanksgiving dinner?"*

3. Explain that Thanksgiving is a holiday to give thanks for family, friends, food, and health.

4. Write the key vocabulary on the board. Define each word by example. Have the students repeat each word.

PRESENTATION

Learn About the Pilgrims

1. Have the students open their books to page 17. Then have them look at the first picture. Ask the students: *"What season is it in the picture? Do the people look happy? What might be wrong?"* If students need a reference for the four seasons, refer them to the illustrations on page 16.

2. After discussing the first picture, read or have students read the corresponding paragraph. Now ask comprehension questions: *"Where were the Pilgrims from? When did they come to America? In what season did the Pilgrims come to America? How did they feel?"*

3. Have the students look at the second picture. Ask them: *"Who is in the picture? What are the people doing? Do they look happy?"*

4. After discussing the second picture, read or have students read the corresponding paragraph. Now ask comprehension questions: *"How did the Indians help the Pilgrims? Why did the Indians and Pilgrims have a big feast? Why do we celebrate Thanksgiving today?"*

Learn About the Pilgrims

In 1620, the Pilgrims came to America from England. They came in the winter. They were cold and hungry.

The Indians helped them find food and build homes. In the fall, the Pilgrims and the Indians had a big feast. They gave thanks for the food. This was the first Thanksgiving.

Listen and Answer

1. What are special holidays in your native country?

2. What do these holidays celebrate?

3. What special foods do you eat on these holidays?

4. What do you do on Thanksgiving Day in the United States?

5. Have you ever been to an American Thanksgiving dinner?

TEACHER'S NOTE: Be sure to discuss each picture in detail. Refer students to the picture of a modern Thanksgiving on page 16.

17

Listen and Answer

The following questions are all for conversation practice. The writing on the board is for reinforcement.

1. Ask the students question 1. Write the names of the countries and the special holidays on the board.

2. Ask question 2. Write one or two words that describe what each holiday celebrates.

3. Ask questions 3-5.

Extension Activities begin on page 56.

PURPOSE

1. To learn that the fourth of July is Independence Day.

2. To talk about independence days in students' native countries.

3. To learn key vocabulary: *independence, Fourth of July, parade, picnic, fireworks,* and *barbecue.*

PREPARATION

1. Show the month of July on a calendar. Circle July 4. Ask students, *"What holiday is this?"*

2. Using a world map, point to the U.S. Ask the students what country this is. Point to England, and ask what country this is. Explain that before 1776 England ruled America. In 1776 the people living in these colonies started to fight for their independence.

3. Write the word *independence* on the board. Use personal or political examples to illustrate the concept of independence.

4. Explain that the Fourth of July is celebrated to honor U.S. independence.

5. Write the key vocabulary on the board. Define each word by illustration or example. Have the students repeat each word.

PRESENTATION

Listen and Answer

1. Have the students open their books to page 18. Then have them look at and discuss the picture at the top of the page. Explain that on the Fourth of July, the flag is displayed and firework shows are presented.

2. After discussing the picture, read the first sentence below it to the students.

3. Ask individual students question 1. Write on the board the names of the other independence days and, if possible, the dates. Follow up with question 2.

4. Ask the students question 3.

5. Talk about each of the pictures under question 4. Explain that people celebrate the Fourth of July by having

Chapter 8
The Fourth of July

Listen and Answer

The Fourth of July is a holiday that celebrates America's independence from England.

1. Does your country celebrate an independence day?
2. How do you celebrate it?
3. Do you celebrate the Fourth of July?
4. Circle how you celebrate the Fourth of July.

picnic

fireworks

parade

barbecue

TEACHER'S NOTE: Use concrete examples of personal and political independence to aid students. Again, introduce new words by using the pictures and labels.

18

parades, picnics, firework shows, and barbecues. Tell the students that many people do not work on the Fourth of July. Since this holiday is in the summer, people like to be outside.

6. Have the students circle the picture(s) that shows how they celebrate the Fourth of July. Ask the students, *"Are there any other ways you celebrate the Fourth of July?"* List them on the board.

Extension Activities begin on page 56.

PURPOSE

1. To learn the story of Independence Day and the American Revolution.

2. To discuss independence in the students' native countries.

3. To learn key vocabulary: *independence, freedom, colonies, Declaration of Independence,* and *the American Revolution.*

PREPARATION

1. Show the month of July on a calendar. Circle July 4. Ask students, *"What holiday is this?"*

2. Tell students that they are going to learn about America's independence. Ask them what *independence* means—for a person and for a country. Write examples on the board.

3. Write the key vocabulary on the board. Define each word by illustration or example. Have the students repeat each word.

PRESENTATION

Learn About American Independence

1. Have the students open their books to page 19. Then have them look at and discuss the picture at the top of the page. Ask them: *"What is happening in the picture? Do you think this picture is from 1989? Why or why not?"*

2. After discussing the picture, read the paragraphs about Independence Day to the students. If students are able, encourage them to read the passage, either silently or out loud.

3. Ask comprehension questions: *"When is Independence Day in the U.S.? In 1776 what country ruled America? What was the name of the war between America and England?"*

Check Yes or No

1. Use the yes-or-no statements to further comprehension. Read the statements, and have the students say *yes* or *no*.

2. Have the students check *yes* or *no* in their books.

Learn About American Independence

The Fourth of July is an important holiday in the U.S. We call this holiday Independence Day to celebrate our freedom.

In 1776, England had 13 colonies in America. The American colonies were not free. The colonists wrote the Declaration of Independence to tell England that they wanted to be free.

The colonies fought a war against England. This war was called the American Revolution. The colonies won and became the United States of America in 1783.

✔ Check Yes or No

1. The American Revolution was fought against Spain. Yes ☐ No ☐

2. We celebrate the Fourth of July to remember U.S. independence. Yes ☐ No ☐

3. My native country celebrates an independence day. Yes ☐ No ☐

TEACHER'S NOTE: Before beginning the reading, explain that the picture shows soldiers fighting in the American Revolution.

19

Extension Activities begin on page 57.

PURPOSE

1. To recognize the name George Washington and the symbols used to remember him.

2. To learn that George Washington was the first president of the United States.

3. To learn key vocabulary: *George Washington, president, remember, memorial,* and *birthday.*

PREPARATION

1. Show the month of February on a calendar. Circle February 22. Ask students, *"What holiday is this?"* Tell them this was George Washington's birthday. George Washington was the first president of the United States. (Show students Washington's picture on a dollar bill.)

2. Explain that after the United States became free from England (after the American Revolution), Americans wanted a new government. George Washington was chosen to be the leader of this new government. He became the first U.S. president.

3. Ask students, *"Who is the president of the United States today?"*

4. Write the key vocabulary on the board. Define each word by illustration or example. Have the students repeat each word.

PRESENTATION

Look and Listen

1. Tell students to open their books to page 20. Then have them discuss the picture of George Washington.

2. After discussing the picture, read the sentences about George Washington to the students.

3. Explain that Washington is called "The Father of His Country" because he was the first president. He helped create a new government for the U.S.

Circle the Memorials to Washington

1. Before doing the circling activity, show the students a dollar bill, a quarter, and both Washington state and Washington, D.C., on a map. Explain

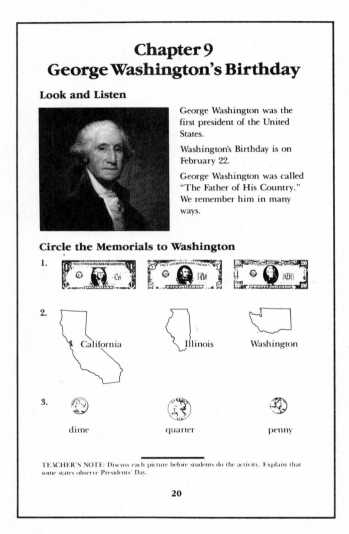

that these things help Americans remember George Washington. They are called memorials.

2. Go over all of the choices individually for question 1. Then have the students tell you which is the memorial to Washington. Do the same for questions 2 and 3.

3. Have the students circle the memorials to Washington in their books, and state what each one is.

Extension Activities begin on page 57.

PURPOSE

1. To give a brief historical sketch of George Washington.

2. To learn to read a timeline.

3. To learn key vocabulary: *leader, revolution, independent, colonies, elect,* and *president.*

PREPARATION

1. Show the month of February on a calendar. Circle February 22. Ask students, *"What holiday is this?"*

2. Ask students, *"Who was George Washington?"* Tell them he was the first president of the United States.

3. Explain to students that in the United States there is a presidential election every four years. The citizens of the United States vote for a new president. (Show the picture of the voting booth from page 40 of the student text.)

4. Ask students, *"Who is now the president of the United States?"* Explain that George Bush is the forty-first president. Show the students his picture on page 32 of their text.

5. Ask students, *"Who is the president of your native country?"*

6. Write the key vocabulary on the board. Define each word by example. Have the students repeat each word.

PRESENTATION

Learn About the First President

1. Have the students open their books to page 21. Then have them look at and discuss the picture at the top of the page.

2. After discussing the picture, read the passage about George Washington to the students. If students are able, encourage them to read the passage, either silently or out loud.

3. Ask students the following comprehension questions: *"Who was George Washington? What country did the colonies want to be independent from? In what year was Washington elected president?"*

Fill in the Timeline

1. Write the timeline on the board. Explain to the students that each date

---

Learn About the First President

We celebrate George Washington's birthday on February 22. The picture shows Washington as the leader of the army in the American Revolution. The American colonies won the war. They became independent from England.

The new country called itself the United States of America. A new government was started. George Washington was elected the first U.S. president in 1789. He helped begin the United States.

Fill in the Timeline

```
 ___            ___                  ___
|_____|_____|__|___
1492            1620                 1776 1789
```

1. The Declaration of Independence was written.

2. Columbus came to America.

3. George Washington was elected president.

4. The first Thanksgiving was celebrated.

TEACHER'S NOTE: First, review information in previous chapters before working with the timeline. Then have the students write the number of the corresponding sentence above the correct year.

21

---

represents an important event that they have studied in this class. Read each of the sentences below the timeline, one at a time. After reading sentence 1, ask the students in what year this event took place. Write 1 above that year. Do the same for sentences 2, 3, and 4.

2. Using the timeline as a jumping-off point, ask the students: *"What happened in 1492? When did the Pilgrims and Indians have the first Thanksgiving? Why is the year 1776 important? Who was elected president in 1789?"*

Extension Activities begin on page 57.

PURPOSE

1. To recognize the name *Abraham Lincoln*.

2. To learn that Lincoln was the sixteenth president of the United States.

3. To recognize the memorials to Lincoln.

4. To learn key vocabulary: *Abraham Lincoln, stamp, penny,* and *five-dollar bill.*

PREPARATION

1. Show the month of February on a calendar. Circle February 12. Ask students, *"What holiday is this?"*

2. Introduce the name *Abraham Lincoln*. Show students his likeness on a penny and a five-dollar bill.

3. Tell the students that he was the sixteenth president of the United States.

4. Write the key vocabulary on the board. Define each word by illustration or example. Have the students repeat each word.

PRESENTATION

Look and Listen

1. Have the students open their books to page 22. Have the students look at and discuss the picture of Abraham Lincoln. Point to the picture. Ask: *"Who is this? What did he do? Have you seen his picture anywhere?"*

2. After discussing the picture, read the sentences next to the picture.

3. Summarize the story of the Civil War on page 23. Use the map to show what is meant by *He kept the U.S. together as 1 country.*

Match the Picture of Lincoln and the Word

1. Bring in a penny and a five-dollar bill. Ask the students what each item is. Tell the students that famous people's faces often appear on these items.

2. Tell the students: *"Lincoln's face is on the penny and the five-dollar bill. Stamps have different pictures on them.*

Chapter 10
Abraham Lincoln's Birthday

Look and Listen

Abraham Lincoln was the sixteenth president of the United States.

He kept the U.S. together as 1 country.

Lincoln's Birthday is on February 12.

Match the Picture of Lincoln and the Word

1. stamp

2. penny

3. $5 bill

TEACHER'S NOTE: Read or summarize the story of the Civil War on page 23 to explain what is meant by "He kept the U.S. together as 1 country."

22

Some stamps have Lincoln's picture on them."

3. Review the pictures and the words in the matching exercise.

4. Have the students first show you which words they will match with which pictures. Then have them do the activity in their books.

Extension Activities begin on page 58.

PURPOSE

1. To learn about Abraham Lincoln and the Civil War.

2. To name two Northern states and two Southern states.

3. To learn key vocabulary: *Abraham Lincoln, sixteenth president, Civil War,* and *slavery.*

PREPARATION

1. Show the month of February on a calendar. Circle February 12. Ask students, *"What holiday is this?"*

2. Give a brief description of the Civil War. Write *1861–1865* on the board. Tell students, *"Abraham Lincoln was president during the Civil War, from 1861 to 1865."*

3. Point to the North and the South on the U.S. map. Tell students, *"The Civil War was a war between the Northern states and the Southern states."*

4. Write the key vocabulary on the board. Define each word by illustration or example. Have the students repeat each word. Define *slavery*: (1) the forcing of people to work for no money and (2) the buying and selling of people.

PRESENTATION

Learn About the Civil War

1. Have the students open their books to page 23. Then have them look at and discuss the map at the top of the page. Discuss how the U.S. was divided during the Civil War. Also, show students how to read the key and the shading on the map.

2. After discussing the map, read the paragraphs about the Civil War and Lincoln to the students. If students are able, encourage them to read the passage, either silently or out loud.

3. Ask comprehension questions: *"Who was Abraham Lincoln? Was the Civil War between the U.S. and England? When was the Civil War? Why was there a war? How did Lincoln die?"*

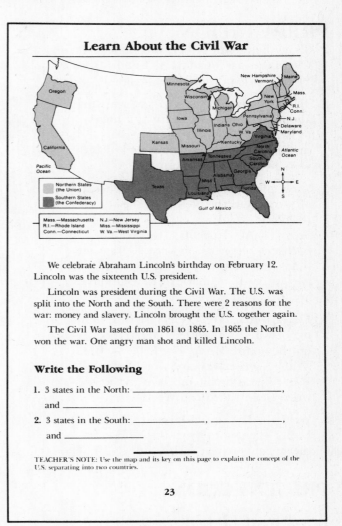

Learn About the Civil War

Northern States (the Union)
Southern States (the Confederacy)

Mass.—Massachusetts   N.J.—New Jersey
R.I.—Rhode Island   Miss.—Mississippi
Conn.—Connecticut   W. Va.—West Virginia

We celebrate Abraham Lincoln's birthday on February 12. Lincoln was the sixteenth U.S. president.

Lincoln was president during the Civil War. The U.S. was split into the North and the South. There were 2 reasons for the war: money and slavery. Lincoln brought the U.S. together again.

The Civil War lasted from 1861 to 1865. In 1865 the North won the war. One angry man shot and killed Lincoln.

Write the Following

1. 3 states in the North: _____, _____, and _____

2. 3 states in the South: _____, _____, and _____

TEACHER'S NOTE: Use the map and its key on this page to explain the concept of the U.S. separating into two countries.

23

Write the Following

1. Let the students work in pairs to identify Northern and Southern states. Have them report their answers orally.

2. Write some of the students' answers on the board as examples. Then have the students write their answers in their books.

Extension Activities begin on page 58.

PURPOSE

1. To understand why the U.S. has a Memorial Day.

2. To learn about different ways that the war dead are honored on Memorial Day.

3. To learn key vocabulary: *honor, soldiers, doctors, nurses, graves,* and *memorials.*

PREPARATION

1. Show the month of May on a calendar. Circle the last Monday. Ask students, *"What holiday is this?"*

2. Tell students that they will be learning about Memorial Day. This is a holiday to remember soldiers and others (medical personnel) who were killed in wars.

3. Show pictures to illustrate the concept of war. (Even the picture of the Revolutionary War on page 19 could be used.) Ask students, *"Was your native country ever in a war?"* Remind them that they have already studied two wars—the American Revolution and the Civil War.

4. Explain that the U.S. has been in four major wars in the 1900s. Write them on the board: *World War I, World War II, the Korean War,* and *the Vietnam War.* (The timeline on page 25 shows when these wars occurred.)

5. Write the key vocabulary on the board. Define each word by example. Have the students repeat each word.

PRESENTATION

Look and Listen

1. Have the students open their books to page 24. Then have them look at and discuss the picture of Arlington National Cemetery at the top of the page. Ask them: *"What is this a picture of? Is it different from most cemeteries? How is it different?"*

2. After discussing the picture, remind students that a memorial is a way to remember someone. (Memorials were discussed in Chapter 9.) Remind students that the cemetery is a memorial to honor the soldiers who died in past wars.

3. Read the description of Memorial Day. Ask students, *"Why does the U.S. have a Memorial Day?"*

Chapter 11
Memorial Day

Look and Listen

On Memorial Day, we honor the soldiers, doctors, and nurses who were killed in American wars.

Listen and Match

1. On Memorial Day, many people do not have to work.

2. Some people visit the graves of loved ones.

3. Some people visit memorials.

TEACHER'S NOTE: Go over the words "soldiers," "doctors," "nurses," "graves," and "memorials." Discuss each picture before beginning the matching exercise.

24

Listen and Match

1. Write each sentence on the board.

2. Read and discuss each sentence with students. Relate each sentence to students' personal experiences. For instance, for sentence 1, ask students, *"Do you have to work on Memorial Day?"*

3. Once people understand the sentences, go over each picture. Ask, *"What does this picture show?"*

4. Work with the students on the matchup activity.

Extension Activities begin on page 58.

PURPOSE

1. To learn about the four major wars that are commemorated on Memorial Day.

2. To read a timeline.

3. To learn key vocabulary: *fought (fight), injured, killed, graves, soldiers,* and *veterans.*

PREPARATION

1. Show the month of May on a calendar. Circle the last Monday. Ask students, *"What holiday is this?"*

2. Use the pictures on the bottom of page 24 to describe different ways that the war dead are honored on Memorial Day.

3. Tell students that they will be learning about Memorial Day: a holiday to honor the memory of soldiers who have died in wars.

4. Make a big timeline on the board from 1900 to the present. Fill in the four major wars discussed in the chapter. Ask the students if they know the dates of major wars in their native countries.

5. Write the key vocabulary on the board. Define each word by example. Have students repeat each word.

PRESENTATION

Learn About the Wars

1. Have the students open their books to page 25, and discuss the picture. Ask them, *"Who are the people in the picture? What are they doing? Who is the parade for?"*

2. Tell the students, *"This is a picture of soldiers who fought in a war; these soldiers are called veterans. They are being honored with a parade."*

3. Read the passage under the picture. If students are able, encourage them to read the passage, either silently or out loud.

Circle Yes or No

1. Read each sentence to the students. Have students tell you *yes* or *no*. If the answer is no, have students correct the statement.

2. Go back over each sentence and have the students circle *yes* or *no* in their books.

Learn About the Wars

In the 1900s, the U.S. fought in 4 major wars. Many American men and women were killed. We honor these men and women on Memorial Day.

Many people do not work on Memorial Day. On that day, they remember the people who were injured or killed. Some people remember with parades. Others remember by visiting the graves of soldiers.

World War I	World War II	Korean War	Vietnam War
1914–1918	1939–1945	1950–1953	1954–1975

Circle Yes or No

1. In the 1900s, the U.S. fought in only 1 war.   Yes No
2. Many people were killed in the wars.   Yes No
3. On Memorial Day, we honor people who were injured or killed in wars.   Yes No
4. Only men were killed in the wars.   Yes No

TEACHER'S NOTE: Explain that the picture shows a memorial parade for soldiers. Also, go over each war on the timeline before beginning the exercise.

25

Extension Activities begin on page 58.

PURPOSE

1. To understand the meaning of Labor Day.

2. To talk about jobs.

3. To learn key vocabulary: *national, honor, workers, Labor Day,* and *job.*

PREPARATION

1. Ask students, *"Do you work?"* Ask each student individually where he works.

2. Write the word *worker* on the board. Show them the root word *work.* Tell them another word for *work* is *labor.*

3. Show the month of September on a calendar. Circle the first Monday in September. Ask students, *"What holiday is this?"*

4. Tell them that the first Monday in September is Labor Day. Ask the students, *"Have you heard of Labor Day? What does Labor Day celebrate? Do you have to work on Labor Day?"*

5. Write the key vocabulary on the board. Define each word by illustration or example. Have the students repeat each word.

PRESENTATION

Listen and Answer

1. Have the students open their books to page 26. Then have them look at and discuss the pictures at the top of the page. For each picture, ask them: *"What workplace do you see? Who are the workers? What are they doing?"*

2. After discussing the pictures, read the sentences about Labor Day. Be sure the concepts of *honor* and *national* are clear.

3. Ask the two questions to individual students.

4. Have students ask each other the questions.

Match the Hat with the Workplace

1. First talk about each hat.

Chapter 12
Labor Day

Listen and Answer

factory   office   restaurant

Labor Day is a national holiday to honor workers.
On Labor Day, most people do not have to work.

1. What is your job?

2. Name 2 good things about your job. Name 2 bad things.

Match the Hat with the Workplace

chef's hat

hard hat

nurse's hat

hospital

restaurant

construction

TEACHER'S NOTE: Discuss all of the pictures of the workplaces at the top of the page. Also, go over the pictures in the matching activity before you start.

26

---

2. Ask the students to guess what type of work the wearer of this hat would do.

3. Ask the students if they wear special hats for their work.

4. Talk about each workplace pictured on the right. Ask students: *"What is this place? What type of work is it? What kind of worker works here?"*

5. Help the students do the matchup activity.

Extension Activities begin on page 59.

PURPOSE

1. To learn the history of Labor Day.

2. To discuss workers' rights.

3. To learn key vocabulary: *workers, unions, workday, money, health insurance, dangerous, safe,* and *workplace.*

PREPARATION

1. Show the month of September on a calendar. Circle the first Monday. Ask students, *"What holiday is this?"*

2. Go over the pictures on page 26. Ask the students, *"What kinds of jobs are shown here?"*

3. Ask students: *"Do you have a job? What is your job? What kind of work would you like to do? Do you belong to a union? What does a union do?"*

4. Write the key vocabulary on the board. Define each word by example. Have the students repeat each word.

PRESENTATION

Learn About Labor Day

1. Have the students open their books to page 27. Then have them look at and discuss the picture. Ask them, *"What are the women doing? Do you think this picture is from the 1980s?"*

2. After discussing the picture, read the paragraphs to the students. If students are able, encourage them to read the passage, either silently or out loud. Read one paragraph at a time, stopping to discuss each.

3. Discuss what is meant by *the 1800s.* Make a list on the board to show the similarities and differences between the 1800s and today. Here is an example.

1800s	1997 (or 1990s)
12-hour workday	7- or 8-hour workday
7-day workweek	5-day workweek
children worked	most don't

Be sensitive that some students' work situations may be similar to the 1800s.

4. Ask the comprehension questions: *"How is Labor Day celebrated? When*

Learn About Labor Day

On Labor Day we celebrate the workers of America. We do this with parades, barbecues, and picnics. Labor Day has been a national holiday since 1894.

Look at the picture of people working in the 1800s. Work was very hard then. Some people worked 15 to 16 hours a day. Many people worked 6 or 7 days a week. Women and children worked for very little money.

Some workers wanted to stop these problems. They got together in unions. The unions helped the people to make their jobs better.

Circle the Things That Help Workers

1. 18-hour workdays   8-hour workdays

2. more money   less money

3. health insurance   no health insurance

4. dangerous workplace   safe workplace

TEACHER'S NOTE: Go over all of the terms before starting the exercise. The concepts of "health insurance" and "dangerous workplace" may be especially challenging. Examples from students' own jobs should prove helpful.

27

---

was the first Labor Day? What were some working conditions in the 1800s? Why did people join unions?"

Circle the Things That Help Workers

1. Discuss each pair of opposites before beginning the exercise.

2. Have the students circle the items that help workers. Check their answers with them.

Extension Activities begin on page 59.

PURPOSE

1. To learn who Martin Luther King, Jr., was.

2. To learn about basic civil rights issues.

3. To learn key vocabulary: *believe(d)*, *school*, *jobs*, *home*, and *vote*.

PREPARATION

1. Show the month of January on a calendar. Circle the third Monday. Ask students, *"What holiday is this?"*

2. Ask the students, *"Have you heard of Martin Luther King, Jr.? Who was he? What did he do?"*

3. Point out Martin Luther King, Jr., in the picture on page 29.

4. Write the words *civil rights* on the board. Define *civil* (for the people or citizens) and *rights* (the privileges and freedoms every resident has).

5. Write the key vocabulary on the board. Define each word by illustration or example. Have the students repeat each word.

PRESENTATION

Match the Words and Pictures

1. Have the students open their books to page 28. Then have them look at and discuss each picture. Ask them, *"What do you see in the picture? Do you work? Do you go to school?"*

2. Go over the words beneath the pictures.

3. Do the matchup activity with the students.

Listen and Answer

1. Read each statement to the students.

2. Ask each question to individual students.

3. Follow up each question with questions about specific examples in students' lives.

4. Have the students work in pairs to ask each other the questions.

Chapter 13
Martin Luther King, Jr., Day

Match the Words and Pictures

1. school   2. vote   3. work   4. home

Listen and Answer

1. Martin Luther King, Jr., believed in good schools for everyone.
   - What do you like about school?

2. Martin Luther King, Jr., believed in good jobs for everyone.
   - Do you have a job?
   - Is it a good job?

3. Martin Luther King, Jr., believed in good homes for everyone.
   - Where do you live?
   - Is it a good place to live?

4. Martin Luther King, Jr., believed that everyone should vote.
   - Would you like to vote in the U.S.?

TEACHER'S NOTE: Go over the pictures and words before starting the matching activity. Follow up the questions with specific examples from students' lives.

28

Extension Activities begin on page 60.

PURPOSE

1. To learn basic information about Martin Luther King, Jr., and the civil rights movement.

2. To understand what the civil rights movement accomplished.

3. To learn key vocabulary: *civil rights, education, housing, jobs, vote (voting), peaceful,* and *march(ing).*

PREPARATION

1. Show the month of January on a calendar. Circle the third Monday. Ask students, *"What holiday is this?"*

2. Go over the pictures on page 28 as an introduction to the key civil rights concepts: *work, housing, school,* and *voting.*

3. Explain that the focus of the lesson will be on a group of people (the workers of the civil rights movement) who worked for equal rights in work, housing, education, and voting. One of the most famous leaders of that movement was Martin Luther King, Jr.

4. Write the key vocabulary on the board. Define each word by illustration or example. Have the students repeat each word.

PRESENTATION

Learn About the Civil Rights Movement

1. Have students open their books to page 29. Then have them look at and discuss the picture at the top of the page. Ask them: *"Where is this? What are these people doing? Why do you think they are marching?"* Point out Martin Luther King, Jr., in the picture.

2. Read the passage out loud. Stop at the end of each paragraph and discuss it. If students are able, encourage them to read the passage, either silently or out loud.

3. Ask the comprehension questions: *"Why was there a civil rights movement? What is meant by peaceful change? When was Martin Luther King, Jr., shot? Why is his birthday celebrated?"*

**Learn About
the Civil Rights Movement**

Martin Luther King, Jr., was a leader of the civil rights movement. The people in the civil rights movement wanted everyone to have equal rights in education, housing, jobs, and voting.

Martin Luther King, Jr., and other people worked very hard for these rights. They worked together for peaceful change. The picture shows King and others marching for change.

In 1968, Martin Luther King, Jr., was shot and killed. We celebrate his birthday to remember his work in civil rights.

Copy the Slogans Under the Headings

| HIRE MORE MINORITIES! | REGISTER TO VOTE! | DON'T RAISE OUR RENT! | MORE TEACHERS! |

Schools _____   **Work** _____

Housing _____   **Voting** _____

TEACHER'S NOTE: Discuss the photo of the civil rights march and what it shows. Be sure to explain the slogans and how to do the exercise. You can use this chapter to have students talk about changes in society they would like to see.

29

Copy the Slogans Under the Headings

1. Read the slogans. Interpret them with the class.

2. Do the exercise orally with the students. Then have the students write the correct slogan under each heading.

3. Go over the answers with the class. Discuss each of the answers.

Extension Activities begin on page 60.

PURPOSE

1. To identify the functions of a president, governor, and mayor.

2. To know the name of the president.

3. To learn key vocabulary: *leader, president, governor,* and *mayor.*

PREPARATION

1. Ask the students: *"What are the names of some famous U.S. presidents? What were they famous for?"* Moving to the state and local levels, ask them: *"What state do you live in? What city do you live in?"*

2. Bring in pictures of their governor and mayor (if applicable). Show the pictures to the students, and ask, *"Who is this?"*

3. Write the key vocabulary on the board. Define each word by illustration or example. Have the students repeat each word.

PRESENTATION

Listen and Choose

1. Have the students open their books to page 32. Then have them look at and discuss the illustrations at the top of the page.

2. Write *president, governor,* and *mayor* on the board. Talk about what each is the leader of.

3. Do the matchups with the students. Then read each statement out loud.

4. Ask questions about each statement, for example, *"Who is the leader of the U.S.?"*

Listen and Answer

1. Ask each question. Point out the picture of the president as you discuss question 1.

2. Write the names of the president, governor, and mayor (if applicable) on the board.

Chapter 14
Important People to Know

Listen and Choose

California

New York

state

United States   city

1. The president is the leader of the _____.
2. The governor is the leader of the _____.
3. The mayor is the leader of the _____.

Listen and Answer

1. This is the president of the United States. What is his name?
2. Who is the governor of your state?
3. Who is the mayor of your city?

TEACHER'S NOTE: Go over the pictures before starting the matching exercise. Also, ask the students about their community leaders. These can include religious leaders, business leaders, or activists.

32

---

3. Expand on the concept of leader by discussing
   a. leaders within the school (principal or director, etc.)
   b. leaders within the community
   c. leaders at the workplace (boss, supervisor, etc.)

4. Ask students, *"Who are the important leaders in your native country?"* Write the name of the country and the leader on the board.

Extension Activities begin on page 61.

PURPOSE

1. To identify important places in the government: the White House, state capitol building, and city hall.

2. To learn where government leaders work.

3. To learn key vocabulary: *president, governor, mayor, White House, capital, capitol,* and *city hall.*

PREPARATION

1. Review the titles and names of key leaders from page 32.

2. Ask the students: *"Where is the capital of the United States? Where is the state capital?"* Write both on the board.

3. If possible, bring in pictures of the mayor (if applicable), the governor, the president, and the vice president. Show the pictures to the students, and discuss the name and position of each person.

PRESENTATION

Learn About Important People and Places

1. Have the students open their books to page 33. Then have them look at and discuss each picture.

2. When discussing the pictures, explain who works at each place, for example, *"President Clinton works in the White House."*

3. Read the passage to the students. If students are able, encourage them to read the passage, either silently or out loud. Pause after each paragraph, and discuss it with students.

4. Ask the comprehension questions: *"Who is the president? Where does he live and work? Who is the vice president? Who is the governor? Where does he work? Who is the mayor (if applicable)? Where does he work?"*

Find the Words

1. Go over the list of words to find. Make sure that students understand the terms.

**Learn About
Important People and Places**

White House

State Capitol Building

City Hall

The president of the United States is Bill Clinton. He lives and works in the White House in Washington, D.C. The vice president is Al Gore.

Every state has a governor. The governor works in the city that is the state capital. Who is the governor of your state?

Cities and towns have mayors. A mayor works in the city hall. Who is the mayor of your city?

Find the Words

D	C	A	P	I	T	A	L	W	A	B
T	I	S	T	O	P	S	T	O	P	S
M	T	M	A	Y	O	R	S	L	O	V
A	Y	T	L	Y	V	S	G	Y	D	D
W	H	I	T	E	H	O	U	S	E	X
B	A	P	R	E	S	I	D	E	N	T
X	L	H	S	T	A	T	E	J	H	V
X	L	G	O	V	E	R	N	O	R	G

CAPITAL
CITY HALL
GOVERNOR
MAYOR
PRESIDENT
STATE
WHITE HOUSE

TEACHER'S NOTE: Go over the pictures at the top of the page before starting the reading. Demonstrate how to do a word find before starting the activity. Explain to the students that the answers go across and up and down.

33

---

2. Demonstrate how to do the word find. Explain that words can be found across or up and down.

3. Tell students to cross out each word as they find it.

4. Help the students check their work.

Extension Activities begin on page 61.

PURPOSE

1. To familiarize students with federal, state, and local laws.

2. To explain why laws are created (to help the government work, to protect people, etc.).

3. To learn key vocabulary: *laws, obey, government, protect,* and *taxes.*

PREPARATION

1. Ask students about the laws (or rules) they are familiar with. You may begin with examples from school, work, and driving.

2. Write the key vocabulary on the board. Define each word by illustration or example. Have the students repeat each word.

3. Discuss with the students the ideas of sales taxes, driving laws, and immunization laws. Be as concrete as possible, for example: *"What is a sales tax? When do you pay it?"* (You may want to show a receipt to illustrate this.) *"Give me an example of a driving law. Why do children need to get shots?"*

PRESENTATION

Listen and Circle the Picture

1. Have the students open their books to page 34. Then have them look at and discuss the pictures. Notice that each picture appears twice. Go over each individual picture (construction worker, inoculation, and car) only once. Ask students, *"What do you see in this picture?"*

2. Read the opening statements. Provide some examples of laws, or draw out more examples from students.

3. Explain the activity. Tell students that they will circle the picture that matches what they hear. Read sentence 1. Wait for students to circle the picture. Repeat for sentences 2 and 3.

Chapter 15
Obeying the Laws

Listen and Circle the Picture
Everyone must obey the laws.
Laws are made to help the government and to protect people.

1. We pay sales taxes to the state. This money is used to build roads and schools.

2. We obey driving laws to protect people's safety.

3. Children must get shots before they go to school. The shots protect children so they do not get sick.

TEACHER'S NOTE: Go over each picture before starting the exercise. Also, encourage students to talk about other laws that they encounter.

34

Extension Activities begin on page 61.

PURPOSE

1. To learn that laws help and protect people.

2. To learn about specific laws.

3. To learn key vocabulary: *law, tax(es), speed limit, accident(s), protect,* and *shot(s)*.

PREPARATION

1. Go over the three different pictures on page 34 of the student text to present different types of laws.

2. Read the opening statements from page 34. Ask students, *"What do you think laws are? Why do we obey laws?"*

3. Write the key vocabulary on the board. Define each word by illustration or example. Have the students repeat each word.

PRESENTATION

Learn About Obeying the Laws

1. Have the students open their books to page 35. Then have them discuss the picture. Ask students: *"What do you see here? Why do you think this happened? What kinds of laws are made to prevent traffic accidents from happening?"*

2. Read the passage to the students. If students are able, encourage them to read the passage themselves, either silently or out loud. Pause after each paragraph, and discuss it with students.

3. Discuss each law described in the passage. Use the pictures on page 34 to illustrate each.

Think and Answer

1. Tell the students that the questions will be asking what they think about different laws.

2. Go over each question, soliciting several different responses.

3. Be sure to encourage and respect differing opinions.

Learn About Obeying the Laws

Some laws help the government to work. For example, we pay sales taxes on what we buy in a restaurant or store. The taxes are used to pay for new roads and schools.

Other laws are also made to protect people. There are traffic laws that set speed limits. These speed limits help to prevent accidents.

There are also special laws to protect children. Children must have certain shots before they can go to school. When they have the shots, children do not catch or pass along some diseases.

Think and Answer

1. What would happen if no one paid taxes?

2. Do laws against speeding do any good? Why or why not?

3. What would happen if children did not get their shots?

TEACHER'S NOTE: Refer to the pictures on page 34 to illustrate the different types of laws discussed in the passage. Also, use the picture at the top of this page to illustrate the consequences of not obeying certain driving laws such as speed limits and stop signs.

35

Extension Activities begin on page 61.

PURPOSE

1. To learn that there are three levels of government.

2. To understand the levels of government that are responsible for different types of laws.

3. To learn key vocabulary: *levels, government, citizenship, marriage, divorce,* and *police.*

PREPARATION

1. Explain that there are three levels of government in the United States. Write each level on the board. Explain that the national (federal) government makes laws for the whole country, a state government makes laws just for that state, and a local government makes laws just for its own area. Use a map to illustrate each level.

2. Write *federal, state,* and *local* on the board. Ask students, *"What are some laws you know about?"* Write each law they mention on the board, under the correct category. If they are all in one category, have some ideas of your own to fill in.

3. Write the key vocabulary on the board. Define each word by illustration or example. Have the students repeat each word.

PRESENTATION

Listen and Match

1. Have the students open their books to page 36.

2. Read the introductory sentences.

3. Ask comprehension questions: *"What are the three levels of government? Do they each make the same types of laws or different ones?"*

4. Go over each of the three pictures. Ask students: *"What do you see in the picture? What is (are) the person (people) doing?"*

5. Read sentences 1-3 several times. Go over the meaning of each sentence.

6. Go back over each sentence, and help the students match it to the appropriate picture.

Chapter 16
Making the Laws

Listen and Match

There are three levels of government.

There is the U.S. government, the state government, and the city government.

They all make different laws.

1. The U.S. government makes laws about citizenship.

2. The state government makes laws about marriage and divorce.

3. The city government makes laws that the police enforce.

TEACHER'S NOTE: Read the sentences to the students. Then discuss what each picture shows before reading the sentences again. Have students match each sentence with the corresponding picture.

36

Extension Activities begin on page 62.

PURPOSE

1. To learn about where laws are made.

2. To learn that laws can be made at the federal, state, and local levels.

3. To learn key vocabulary: *law, federal, Congress, Senate, House of Representatives, city council,* and *local.*

PREPARATION

1. Ask the students, *"Can you name any laws?"* Have some familiar examples prepared in case students need prompting.

2. Refer students back to the pictures at the top of page 32. Tell them, *"We have laws that are for the whole country, laws that are different for each state, and laws for each city."*

3. Write the key vocabulary on the board. Define each word by illustration or example. Have the students repeat each word.

PRESENTATION

Learn About Where the Laws Are Made

1. Have the students open their books to page 37. Then have them look at the picture at the top of the page. Ask them: *"What do you see in the picture? What do you think goes on in this building?"* Tell them: *"This is where the laws are made for the whole United States. This is the U.S. Capitol Building."*

2. After discussing the picture, read the passage out loud. Stop at the end of each paragraph and discuss it. If students are able, encourage them to read the passage, either silently or out loud.

3. Ask the comprehension questions: *"What kind of laws are made for the whole United States? Who makes these laws? What are the two parts of the U.S. Congress? Who makes laws for the state? Who makes laws for cities? What are these laws called?"*

Learn About
Where the Laws Are Made

Laws that are made for the whole United States are called federal laws. The U.S. Congress in Washington, D.C., makes federal laws. The U.S. Congress is made up of two parts: the Senate and the House of Representatives.

Each state has a legislature that is elected to make state laws. Most state legislatures have both a state senate and state house of representatives.

A city council or village board makes local laws.

Circle Yes or No

1. Federal laws are made by the U.S. Congress.	Yes	No
2. State laws are made by the U.S. Congress.	Yes	No
3. Every state has both a senate and a house of representatives.	Yes	No
4. Local laws are made by city councils or village boards.	Yes	No

TEACHER'S NOTE: Tell students that the picture shows the U.S. Capitol building, where federal laws are made. Be sure to review the words "every" and "most" before starting the exercise.

37

Circle Yes or No

1. Before beginning the exercise, define the words *every* and *most.* Use examples if necessary.

2. Have students answer the statements orally. Then tell them that they are now going to circle *yes* or *no* after each sentence is read to them.

3. Read each statement, pausing after each one so that students can circle their answers. Repeat the statements when necessary.

Extension Activities begin on page 62.

PURPOSE

1. To learn basic information about the court system.

2. To identify key people in a courtroom.

3. To learn key vocabulary: *courtroom, judge, jury, guilty, crime, punish(ed), lawyer,* and *witness.*

PREPARATION

1. Review the concept of laws covered in Chapters 15 and 16. Ask students to name some laws they have already learned about.

2. Ask, *"What happens if a law is broken?"*

3. Explain that the purposes of the American court system are (1) to solve problems peacefully and (2) to punish people who have broken laws.

4. Write the key vocabulary on the board. Define each word by illustration or example. Have the students repeat each word.

PRESENTATION

Look and Listen

1. Have the students open their books to page 38. Then have them look at and discuss the picture. Ask students: *"Who do you see in the picture? Where are they?"*

2. Now define each person's role in the picture. (Explain that U.S. citizens are required to serve on juries.) Also tell students about two people not listed—defendant and prosecutor.

3. Read the introductory sentences. Define *guilty of a crime* and *punishment.* Give an example. Crime: driving sixty-eight miles per hour in a fifty-five mile-per-hour zone. What is the law?—fifty-five mile-per-hour speed limit. What is the punishment?—speeding ticket and fine.

Look at the Picture

1. Have the students perform tasks 1-4.

2. Have them point to each of the lettered people in the picture, name the person, and describe his/her role. Students may need help in describing the roles.

Chapter 17
The Courts

Look and Listen

This is a courtroom.

In a courtroom, a judge or jury decides if a law has been broken.

If people are found guilty of a crime, they are punished.

Look at the Picture

1. Find the letter A. This is a lawyer.
2. Find the letter B. This is a judge.
3. Find the letter C. This is a jury.
4. Find the letter D. This is a witness.

Listen and Answer

1. What are some laws in your community?
2. Have you ever gotten a ticket? What was it for?
3. Have you ever been to court? Talk about it.

TEACHER'S NOTE: When finding the lawyer, judge, jury, and witness in the picture, describe to students what each one does.

38

Listen and Answer

1. Read each question. Have individual students answer.

2. Have students ask each other the questions.

3. If students seem reluctant to talk about past experiences in this case, share experiences you might have had or read about in a newspaper.

Extension Activities begin on page 62.

PURPOSE

1. To learn about the Constitution.

2. To learn that the Constitution is the highest law in the United States.

3. To learn key vocabulary: *Constitution, Supreme Court, traffic court,* and *criminal court.*

PREPARATION

1. Remind students about the American Revolution (Chapters 8 and 9). Tell them that when the Americans won their freedom, they made a set of rules for the whole United States. These rules became known as the Constitution. The Constitution is still the basic law of the United States, but it has been changed in some important ways over the past 200 years. Use an example of the voting amendments from page 41 to illustrate this point.

2. Ask students, *"Does your native country have a constitution?"*

3. Explain that there are many types of courts in the United States. Ask students, *"What types of courts are in the United States?"* Tell students that the highest court is the Supreme Court. This court makes sure all laws agree with the Constitution.

4. Write the key vocabulary on the board. Explain each word by illustration or example. Have the students repeat each word.

PRESENTATION

Learn About the Constitution

1. Have the students open their books to page 39. Then have them look at and discuss what they see in the pictures. Ask them: *"Which picture shows the Constitution? Who are the people in the picture?"*

2. Read the passage to the students two or three times. Pause after each paragraph and discuss it with students. If students are able, encourage them to read the passage, either silently or out loud.

3. Ask the comprehension questions: *"What is the basic law of the United*

Learn About the Constitution

The Supreme Court

The Constitution is the basic law of the United States. It was written in 1787. We have many other laws to protect the country and its people. All laws must agree with the Constitution.

The most important court in the United States is the Supreme Court. The 9 judges of the Supreme Court decide if laws agree with the Constitution. There are also other kinds of courts in the U.S. For example, there are traffic courts and criminal courts.

Listen and Answer

1. The minimum wage is $3.35 an hour. Mr. Smith hires José for $3.00 an hour. Who is breaking the law? What might happen?

2. The speed limit is 55 miles per hour. Ann is driving at 67 miles per hour. Is Ann breaking the law? What might happen?

3. The Constitution gives people the right to freedom of speech. Mayor James tries to stop the Equal Rights Group from having a meeting. Who is breaking the law? What might happen?

TEACHER'S NOTE: Go over the questions slowly. Be sure to define terms such as "minimum wage," "speed limit," and "freedom of speech."

39

States? When was the Constitution written? What is the highest court in the United States? Name two other kinds of courts."

Listen and Answer

1. Tell students that you are going to read about three problems. They are to tell you if the person is breaking the law and what might happen to him/her.

2. Read each situation slowly. Be sure to define difficult terms. For each, ask: *"What law is being broken? Who broke the law? What might happen?"*

Extension Activities begin on page 62.

PURPOSE

1. To learn about who is eligible to vote.

2. To look at issues that U.S. citizens vote on.

3. To learn key vocabulary: *right, citizens, register,* and *resident.*

PREPARATION

1. Create a situation in the class for students to vote on. Provide an issue for the students to vote on, for example, *"What time should we take a break?"* Give the students two or three choices, have them vote, and follow the decision.

2. Ask the students, *"How many of you voted in your native countries?"* Have them discuss past voting.

3. Ask, *"How many of you would like to vote in the United States someday?"* Find out if anyone knows the requirements for voting.

4. Write the key vocabulary on the board. Define each word by illustration or example. Have the students repeat each word.

PRESENTATION

Look and Listen

1. Have the students open their books to page 40. Then have them look at and discuss the picture at the top of the page. Ask them: *"What do you see in the picture? Why are the people there?"*

2. After discussing the picture, describe the voting process—going into a booth, using secret ballot, pulling a lever or punching a card, etc.

3. Read over the requirements for voting. Read one at a time, and ask: *"Are you eighteen years old or older? Are you a citizen? Are you registered to vote? Are you a resident of the state?"*

Circle What You Would Vote For

1. Look at the three pairs of issues. Talk about each choice, and have students circle the choices they would support.

Chapter 18
Voting

Look and Listen

Citizens of the United States have the right to vote.

People can vote if they are:

- 18 years old or older
- citizens of the United States
- registered to vote
- residents of their state for at least 30 days

Circle What You Would Vote For

guns   no guns   smoking   no smoking

Clinton   Dole

TEACHER'S NOTE: Discuss each pair of opposites before starting the circling activity. Explain that Michael Dukakis and George Bush were presidential candidates in 1988.

40

---

2. Now have students cast secret ballots on each issue. Go over each issue, one at a time, and have students simply write *yes* or *no* (or *Y* or *N*) on a piece of paper. Collect and count the ballots, and write the results for each vote on the board. Read each result out loud.

Extension Activities begin on page 63.

PURPOSE

1. To follow the development of voting rights.

2. To see the connection between civil rights and voting rights.

3. To learn key vocabulary: *discriminate, Constitution, only, white, nonwhite, special, poor,* and *amendment.*

PREPARATION

1. Have students vote on one issue at the bottom of page 40 of the student text. Set up certain restrictions. (Make sure that students understand this is for demonstration purposes only so that no one feels discriminated against. For example, the first time, no men can vote. The second time, no women can vote.)

2. Discuss this activity. Explain that when you left out certain people you were discriminating. (Write *discriminate* on the board.) Ask people, *"How did you feel when you couldn't vote?"* Explain that the lesson is about changes to end discrimination in voting laws.

3. Write the key vocabulary on the board. Define each word by example. Have the students repeat each word.

PRESENTATION

Learn About Voting Laws

1. Have the students open their books to page 41. Then have them discuss the pictures above the timeline. Ask students: *"What does this person look like? Is it a man or a woman? Is he/she young or old?"*

2. After discussing the pictures, go over the timeline. Explain that when the Constitution was first written, only white men twenty-one years old or older could vote. Tell students that there were changes (amendments) made to the Constitution so more people could vote. Write the word *amendment* on the board.

3. Read the passage to the students two or three times. Pause after each paragraph, and discuss it with students. If students are able, encourage them to read the passage, either silently or out loud.

Learn About Voting Laws

U.S. Constitution	Amendment 15	Amendment 19	Amendment 26
1789	1870	1920	1971
White men 21 years old or older could vote.	Black men could vote.	Women could vote.	The voting age was lowered to 18.

When the United States was started, only white men could vote. This was not fair, so the Constitution was changed. Because of the changes, all adults 18 years old or older can vote. This includes whites and nonwhites, men and women.

During the 1960s, special laws were made to help people to vote. One new law was made so that people did not have to pay to vote. This helped poor people. Another law was made so that people could vote even if they could not read very well. Now all of these people have the right to vote.

✔ **Check Yes or No**

1. Only men can vote.   Yes ☐ No ☐
2. People who are 18 years old can vote.   Yes ☐ No ☐
3. Only rich people can vote.   Yes ☐ No ☐
4. Since the Constitution was changed, more people can vote.   Yes ☐ No ☐

TEACHER'S NOTE: Go over the timeline of amendments at the top of the page to explain how voting laws have changed. Be sure to explain the word "only" before starting the exercise.

41

Check Yes or No

1. Tell students you will read four sentences to them. They are to check *yes* or *no* after each sentence. Demonstrate if necessary.

2. Read through the statements one by one.

3. Discuss each one. Make sure students understand the word *only* before they answer the questions.

4. Help students answer the questions. Have them support their answers with facts from the reading. Check their answers.

Extension Activities begin on page 63.

PURPOSE

1. To recognize famous American symbols.

2. To know the significance of these symbols.

3. To learn key vocabulary: *symbol, represent, Pledge of Allegiance, freedom, independence,* and *immigrants.*

PREPARATION

1. Talk about *symbols* as a way to remember something. Remind students about the memorials to Washington and Lincoln that they learned about on pages 20 and 22.

2. Bring in some other symbols from magazine ads: McDonalds' golden arches, trademarks of famous cars, etc. Tell students they see symbols every day.

3. Write the key vocabulary on the board. Define each word by illustration or example. Have the students repeat each word.

PRESENTATION

Match the Symbol and the Words

1. Have the students open their books to page 42. Then have them look at and discuss each picture. Ask them, *"What is this a picture of?"*

2. Go over each picture in detail. Identify the symbol. Ask students if they have ever seen the symbol. Find out if they saw it in person or in pictures.

3. Read each sentence.

4. Explain to students that they will match each sentence with a picture.

5. Help the students match the words and pictures.

6. Tell the students that the Statue of Liberty is in New York and the Liberty Bell is in Philadelphia. Ask students, *"Where do you see the American flag?"*

Chapter 19
American Symbols

Match the Symbol and the Words

These symbols represent the United States and its history.

—— American flag

—— Statue of Liberty   —— Liberty Bell

1. Pledge of Allegiance and freedom
2. The American Revolution and independence
3. Welcoming immigrants to the U.S.

TEACHER'S NOTE: Discuss each symbol before starting the matching activity. Explain to students where each of these symbols can be seen.

42

Extension Activities begin on page 63.

PURPOSE

1. To recognize key American symbols.

2. To understand the significance of these symbols.

3. To learn key vocabulary: *Statue of Liberty, political freedom, opportunity, immigrants, world friendship,* and *freedom.*

PREPARATION

1. Have students look at the pictures on page 42. Read:

    "In 1777 the American flag became the symbol for freedom in the United States. The flag is red, white, and blue. The red is for courage, the white is for truth, and the blue is for justice.

    "The Liberty Bell is a symbol of the American Revolution. On July 4, 1776, the bell rang when the Declaration of Independence was signed.

    "The Statue of Liberty was a gift from France in 1886. It is a symbol of political freedom, opportunity, and world friendship."

2. Ask students: *"What does the flag of your native country look like? What does that flag mean? What other famous symbols does your country have?"*

3. Write the key vocabulary on the board. Define each word by example. Have the students repeat each word.

PRESENTATION

Learn About American Symbols

1. Have the students open their books to page 43. Then have them look at and discuss the picture. Ask them: *"What do you see in the picture? What is the symbol?"*

2. Read through the first paragraph. If students are able, encourage them to read the passage, either silently or out loud. Ask the comprehension questions: *"What does the Statue of Liberty stand for? Where is it?"*

3. After reading through the second paragraph, ask: *"What colors are on the American flag? How many stars are on it? How many stripes?"*

Learn About American Symbols

The picture shows the Statue of Liberty. It is a symbol of political freedom and opportunity for immigrants. It is also a symbol of world friendship. The statue welcomes many people who come to America to start a new life. It is in New York City, New York.

The American flag is the symbol for freedom in the U.S. The flag is red, white, and blue. The 13 stripes represent the first 13 colonies. The 50 stars represent the 50 states.

The Liberty Bell is a symbol of the American Revolution. On July 4, 1776, the bell rang when the Declaration of Independence was signed. The Liberty Bell is in Philadelphia, Pennsylvania.

Answer the Questions

1. What does the Statue of Liberty mean to new immigrants to America?

2. Where have you seen the American flag?

3. Where can you see the Liberty Bell?

TEACHER'S NOTE: Use the pictures on page 42 to illustrate the three symbols. Have students discuss some symbols of their native countries.

43

---

4. After reading through the third paragraph, ask: *"What does the Liberty Bell stand for? Where is it found?"*

Answer the Questions

1. Read each question to the students.

2. Go back over them one by one. Have students answer each question orally.

3. Ask students if they have seen any of the symbols. If they have, ask them where they saw the symbols.

Extension Activities begin on page 63.

PURPOSE

1. To understand the rights of a permanent resident.

2. To understand the additional rights of a citizen.

3. To learn key vocabulary: *permanent resident* and *naturalized citizen.*

PREPARATION

1. Tell students that they are going to hear two stories. One is about a permanent resident, and the other is about a citizen of the U.S. Ask students: *"How many of you want to become permanent residents? How many would like to become citizens someday? Why or why not?"* (Keep an open mind regarding their answers.)

2. Write the key vocabulary on the board. Define each word by illustration or example. Have the students repeat each word. Also add two terms not in the reading: *temporary resident* and *refugee.* (Define both and explain.)

PRESENTATION

Look and Listen

1. Have the students open their books to page 44. Then have them look at and discuss each picture. Ask them: *"Who do you see in the picture? Where do you think he/she is from?"*

2. Read about Katrina Amado. Have the students find Guatemala on the world map on pages 48–49 of their books.

3. Ask comprehension questions about Katrina: *"Where is Katrina from? Where does Katrina live now? Is Katrina a citizen of the U.S.? Where is Katrina's family? What country does Katrina work in?"*

4. Read about Jan Solasky to the students. Have the students find Poland on the world map on pages 48–49 of their books.

5. Ask comprehension questions about Jan: *"Where is Jan from? Is Jan a citizen of the U.S.? Where is Jan's family? Can Jan vote in the U.S.? What country does Jan work in?"*

Chapter 20
Permanent Residency and Citizenship

Look and Listen

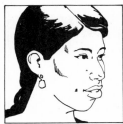 

My name is Katrina Amado. I am a permanent resident of the United States. I am a citizen of my native country, Guatemala. I hope to return to Guatemala some day to see my family. As a permanent resident, I can live and work in the U.S.

My name is Jan Solasky. I am from Poland. I am a naturalized citizen of the United States. I brought my family to the U.S. last year. I wanted them to become U.S. citizens, too. As a citizen, I can live, work, and vote in the U.S. My family can live here, too.

Listen and Circle Yes or No

1. A permanent resident can vote.	Yes	No
2. A naturalized citizen can bring his or her family to the U.S.	Yes	No
3. A permanent resident can remain a citizen of his or her native country.	Yes	No
4. A naturalized citizen is born in the U.S.	Yes	No

TEACHER'S NOTE: Before beginning the activity, make sure that students are clear on the differences between permanent residency and citizenship.

44

Listen and Circle Yes or No

1. Before beginning the activity, make sure each student understands the difference between permanent residency and citizenship.

2. Explain to students that they are to circle *yes* or *no* after hearing each sentence.

3. Read each statement with the class. Wait for students to circle *yes* or *no*, then check their responses.

Extension Activities begin on page 64.

PURPOSE

1. To learn the general requirements for becoming a U.S. citizen.

2. To practice answering the questions that might be asked in a citizenship test.

3. To learn key vocabulary: *naturalized citizen, legal resident,* and *oath of allegiance.*

PREPARATION

1. Review the different legal statuses of people living in the U.S.:
   a. citizens by birth and naturalized citizens
   b. permanent residents
   c. temporary residents
   d. refugees

2. Write the key vocabulary on the board. Define each word by illustration or example. Have the students repeat each word.

PRESENTATION

Learn About Becoming a U.S. Citizen

1. Have the students open their books to page 45. Then have them look at and discuss the picture at the top of the page. Ask them: *"Who are the people in the picture? What do you think they are doing?"*

2. Go through the requirements for becoming a citizen. Read one at a time and discuss what each requirement means.

3. Ask comprehension questions: *"To become a citizen, how old must you be? How long must you have lived in the U.S.? Do you have to take a test? What is the test about?"*

4. Tell students that the questions at the bottom of page 45 are similar to some questions on the citizenship test. Read the questions to the students. Have the students practice asking and answering these questions in pairs.

**Learn About
Becoming a U.S. Citizen**

Requirements for Becoming a Citizen

To become a naturalized citizen, a person must:

- be at least 18 years old
- have lived in the U.S. as a legal resident for at least 5 years (3 years if the person is married to a U.S. citizen)
- be able to read, write, speak, and understand basic English
- have a basic knowledge and understanding of the history, government structure, and the Constitution of the U.S.
- be willing to take an oath of allegiance to the U.S.

Answer the Questions

Practice asking and answering these questions with another student.

1. Who was the first U.S. president?
2. Who was Abraham Lincoln?
3. Who is the U.S. president now?
4. Who is the governor of your state?
5. What is the capital of your state?
6. Describe the American flag.

TEACHER'S NOTE: Use this activity to refresh students' memories about some basic issues in American history and government.

45

Extension Activities begin on page 64.

Extension Activities

CHAPTER 1

Literacy Level
Page 2

1. Write the sentences about Monica on the board. Erase the key vocabulary words:

   My _____ is Monica Gonzales.

   My _____ is 127 W. Monroe Street.

   I _____ in Chicago, Illinois.

   Encourage students to guess the correct words and write them in the blanks.

2. Explain that addresses may have *N., S., E.,* or *W.* as part of the street name. (For reading a compass, see the teacher's notes to Chapter 2 on page 13 of this guide.) Refer to the *W.* in *W. Monroe St.* Show the correlation of *N.* to *North,* etc. If possible, use street names from the students' city to show other examples of how the abbreviations are used.

3. Explain how there are different names for streets used in addresses: *road, street, avenue, boulevard,* etc. Again, use examples from the students' addresses or local street names to demonstrate this. Teach the abbreviations that go with each name: *Road = Rd.; Street = St.; Avenue = Ave.;* and *Boulevard = Blvd.* Have the students say and write their own street addresses.

4. Provide the students with a worksheet. On each line, give three possible street addresses. Say one orally, and have the students circle the address they hear. Below is an example. It would be best to make your own worksheet, using the names and address numbers in your city.
   a. 123 W. Adams   234 E. Adams
      430 N. Adams
   b. 1109 N. Clark   2324 S. Clark
      3216 W. Clark
   c. 434 Main St.   1612 Main St.
      231 Main St.

5. The following activity is a **matchup**. See page 66 for a description of matchups. Make

matchup cards using the following words and phrases.

Words:

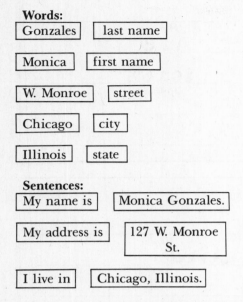

Gonzales   last name

Monica   first name

W. Monroe   street

Chicago   city

Illinois   state

Sentences:

My name is   Monica Gonzales.

My address is   127 W. Monroe St.

I live in   Chicago, Illinois.

Begin with the information about Monica. Then make matchup cards with information about the students in the class.

Beginning Level
Page 3

1. Give each student a blank form similar to the ones on page 3 of the student text. Students should work in pairs and ask their partners the questions needed to fill out the form. Another possibility is to have students make their own forms. This will provide reinforcement for the terms they are working with.

2. The following activity is a **matchup**. See page 66 for a description of matchups. Make large flash cards with the names of cities, states, and countries from the student text as well as the names of students' native cities, states, and countries. The students turn the cards over on a table. One at a time, have students try to match a city, state, and country. This game can also be played as a concentration game. (See page 66 for directions on concentration.) Students can work in small groups, pairs, or individually. An example appears in the box below.

3. For students who have a hard time understanding the words *male* and *female*, put the following headings on the board, and list each student under the proper category.

man/male   woman/female

4. The following activity is an **information gap**. See page 66 for a description of information gaps. This can be done in pairs. (It can also be done with the students having one form and the teacher having the other form.)

    Explain to the students that they are going to fill in a form about Liu Trung. In each pair, one student has half of the information about Liu Trung, and the other student has the other half. Student A is to ask Student B questions in order to fill in the missing information. If students require help in spelling, use Appendix 8 on pages 54–55 of the student text. Here are some sample questions.

> *"What is her first name?"*
> *"How do you spell it?"*
> *"What is the name of her street?"*
> *"How do you spell it?"*
> *"What state does she live in?"*
> *"How do you spell it?"*
> *"Is she male or female?"*
> *"How old is she?"*

Student B answers the questions, then asks his own.

> *"What is her last name?"*
> *"What is her street address?"*
> *"What city does she live in?"*
> *"What is the zip code?"*

After they have both completed their forms, the students exchange forms and check for correct information.

    Sample forms are on page 52.

City	State	Country
Rodeo	Durango	Mexico
Chicago	Illinois	United States

Student A Sample Form

Name: _____ Trung _____ ___—___
(Last)   (First)   (Middle)

Address: _____ 4204 _____ 12 B
(Number)   (Street)   (Apt.#)

_____ Denver _____ 80202
(City)   (State)   (Zip Code)

Sex: ☐ Male   Age: _____

☐ Female   Signature: _____

Student B Sample Form

Name: _____ Liu _____
(Last)   (First)   (Middle)

Address: _____ North Clark Street
(Number)   (Street)   (Apt.#)

_____ Colorado _____
(City)   (State)   (Zip Code)

Sex: ☐ Male   Age: _____ 29

☒ Female   Signature: _____

CHAPTER 2

Literacy Level
Page 4

1. Show the abbreviation for the state the students live in.

2. Explain the possible abbreviations for the United States: U.S. or U.S.A.

3. Using a wall map of the United States, ask the students direction questions such as: *"Is Sacramento north of San Francisco? Is Los Angeles south of Sacramento?"* (You can expand on these questions as desired.)

4. Using a wall map, point to the state students live in. For example, ask the students: *"Is _____ north of Texas? Is _____ south of Texas? Is _____ east of Texas? Is _____ west of Texas?"*

   Encourage students to use complete sentences in the affirmative and the negative.

5. Write personal identification questions on strips of paper: *What is your first name? What is your last name? What is your address? What city do you live in? What state do you live in? Where are you from?*

   Put these questions into a box. Call up one student at a time. Ask the student to pull a question out of the box. Then ask the student the question. The student should respond about himself. Also, students can ask these questions of classmates.

Beginning Level
Page 5

1. Write the names of the students' native countries on the board. Ask students if their countries are divided into states or provinces. Write *yes* or *no*.

2. Ask students the name of their native country's capital, for example, *"What is the capital of Guatemala?"* Write the name of the city next to the name of the country. Here is an example.

Country	Capital	States/ Provinces
Guatemala	Guatemala City	yes
Haiti	Port-au-Prince	no
Mexico	Mexico City	yes

3. Use numbers 1 and 2 as a basis for a speaking activity. Ask questions such as: *"What is the capital of Guatemala? How many countries are divided into states? Mexico City is the capital of what country?"*

4. Using a wall map of the United States, have individual students perform the following tasks:
   a. Point to the country north of the U.S. *"What country is this?"* (Canada.) *"What is the capital of Canada?"* (Ottawa.)
   b. Point to the country south of the U.S. *"What country is this?"* (Mexico.) *"What is the capital of Mexico?"* (Mexico City.)
   c. Point to the state north of your state.
   "What state is this? What is the capital?"
   d. Point to the state south of your state. *"What is the name of this state? What is the capital?"*
   e. Point to the state east of your state, etc.

5. Show how the U.S. is divided into regions— West, East, Midwest, and South. Name one state in each region, and ask the students to name one other state in each region.

CHAPTER 3

Literacy Level
Page 6

1. Ask students the names of their native countries. Write the names on the board. Have the students point to each country on the world map on pages 48–49 of the student text.

2. The following is a **chart** activity. See page 66 for a description of chart activities. Write a chart on the board like the one below. Use Merilee LaRue as an example. Fill her name in on the chart. Ask students: *"What country is she from? Is the country large or small? What city is she from? Is Port-au-Prince a large city or a small city?"* Ask the students the same questions about themselves and fill in the chart with their responses.

Name	Native Country	Size	City	Size
Merilee	Haiti	small	Port-au-Prince	large
(your student)	_____	_____	_____	_____

Beginning Level
Page 7

1. The following is a **chart** activity. See page 66 for a description of chart activities. Write the chart at the bottom of the page on the board. Ask the students to name two countries from each continent. Fill in the chart with their responses. (Remind students that Mexico and Central America are part of North America.) Add students' native countries to the chart.

2. The following activity is a **matchup**. See page 66 for a description of matchups. Make four category cards on 5x8-inch index cards. Use the categories listed below. Write each category in a different colored marker or pencil. Place the four category cards at the top of a table.

city   state   country   continent

    Make individual index cards for the names of the cities, states, countries, and continents the students have seen thus far. Place those index cards, shuffled, in a pile. Have one student at a time turn over the top card of the pile, say the name aloud (with teacher guidance), and place the card under the correct category. This activity can be done in small groups, pairs, or individually.

CHAPTER 4

Literacy Level
Page 8

1. The following activity is a **lineup**. See page 67 for a description of lineups. Call the students to the front of the room. (If your class is too large, call ten students up at a time.) Ask the students to say when they came to the U.S. Have them write the dates on a piece of paper. Then, instruct the students to line up in the order of when

they came to the U.S. The person who came first begins the line on the far left; the person who came last ends the line on the far right.

2. The following is a **timeline** activity. See page 66 for a description of timelines. Make a timeline on the board. Fill in the years people came to the U.S. on the timeline, with their names written above.

José   Maria   Young Cho

1952   1965   1976

————————————————————→

1940   1950   1960   1970   1980   1990

3. Use this timeline as a jumping-off point for oral language practice: *"How many people came to the U.S. in 19____? Did (name of student) come to the U.S. before (name of student)?"*

Beginning Level
Page 9

1. On a world map, make a line with yarn for each student, showing it stretching from their native country to the U.S. Label each line with the name of the student.

2. Have the students bring in a picture of themselves, or use a self-developing camera to take pictures of the students. Students can glue their pictures on pieces of paper and copy the sentences about themselves from Write About Yourself. These can be posted around the room.

3. Bring in different pictures of ethnic and racial groups in America. Post each picture with a name tag next to it: Black American, American Indian, Caucasian, Hispanic, Polish, Japanese, etc.

    These pictures and labels could also be the basis for a **matchup** activity. See page 66 for a description of matchups.

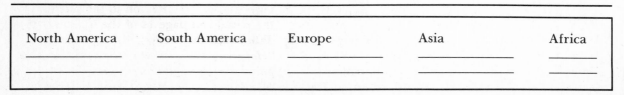

North America	South America	Europe	Asia	Africa
_____	_____	_____	_____	_____
_____	_____	_____	_____	_____

CHAPTER 5

Literacy Level
Page 12

1. Ask students to give their birth dates (month and day). Write the dates on the board. Ask students to circle their birthdays on the calendar on page 12 in their books.

2. Obtain a small calendar book for each student. (These can often be obtained free at local card shops or bookstores.) Have the students mark their classmates' birthdays on their calendars. First review by asking a student, *"When is your birthday?"*, and having that student answer, *"My birthday is _____."*

3. Have students do more practice with dates. Write the names of the months on the board, and number them in order one through twelve. Write a student's birthday on the board like this:

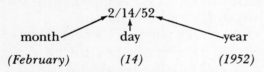

   month   day   year

   (February)   (14)   (1952)

4. Write other dates (including birthdays) in that form, and have students tell you the month, day, and year.

5. Dictate different dates to the students, and have them write the date in the form that you choose.

6. Explain that different forms of numbers are used to say dates. Teach first through thirty-first. Use the list of cardinal and ordinal numbers in Appendix 2 on page 47 of the student text. Have the students practice saying dates.

7. Have the students learn the months and days as sight words. They should also learn the order of the months and days.

8. The following is a **sequencing** activity. See page 67 for a description of sequencing. Make flash cards out of the months and days. Divide the students into groups. Have one group put the months in order. In another group, have the students put the days in order.

9. The following activity is a **lineup**. See page 67 for a description of lineups. Assign individual month cards to twelve different students. Have them align themselves in

order in front of the class. Do the same exercise with the days of the week.

Beginning Level
Page 13

1. Make sure that students know the names of the months and the days of the week.

2. On a wall calendar, circle all of the holidays listed on page 13 of the student text. Extend yarn from each circled date. Write out the names of the holidays in dark, bold print on flash cards, for example, *THANKSGIVING*. Call on individual students to tape the correct holiday to the end of the yarn extending from the date.

3. Ask the students if they know of any other holidays celebrated in the U.S. Write the names of these holidays on the board and the dates they are celebrated. Give a brief description of each holiday.

4. Go through month by month and ask what is celebrated in each month. These may include students' birthdays and/or holidays celebrated in other countries.

5. Illustrate the difference between the words *before* and *after*. You can use numbers or the names of the months or days to do this. Then ask students questions such as: *"What month is before October? What month is after February?"*

6. Activities 3–6 for the literacy level students are also recommended for beginning level students.

CHAPTER 6

Literacy Level
Page 14

1. Ask students who work if they have a day off for Columbus Day. Ask students who are parents if their children go to school on Columbus Day.

2. Direct students' attention to the picture of the parade on page 14 of the student text. Talk about the picture. Ask the students, *"Have you ever been to a parade? Are there parades in your native country? What are the parades for?"*

Beginning Level
Page 15

1. The following is a **story retelling**. See page 67 for a description of story retelling. Ask individual students to retell the story of Columbus, using the pictures and map on pages 14 and 15.

2. Write the following sentences on the board or on a worksheet. Ask the students to answer *yes* or *no*.

   a. People (Indians) were already living in America.

      yes   no

   b. In 1492 Columbus came to America.

      yes   no

   c. Columbus sailed to India.

      yes   no

   d. We celebrate Columbus Day on November 12.

      yes   no

CHAPTER 7

Literacy Level
Page 16

1. On the board, write the information about the students from their responses to Circle Your Answer.

   Name: José
   Year Came to the U.S.: 1962
   Season: winter
   Lived: in an apartment with my brother

   Use this as a jumping-off point for a speaking activity. Ask students: *"How many people came in the winter? How many people lived with someone in their family?"*

2. Have the students complete the following sentence, *"I am thankful for _____, _____, _____, and _____."*

Beginning Level
Page 17

1. The following is a **sequencing** activity. See page 67 for a description of sequencing. Write the seven sentences from page 17 of the student text on strips of paper. Divide the class into small groups. Pass a complete set of strips out to each group. Have them arrange the sentences in the correct order.

2. Have the students write in their small calendars or on the class wall calendar the names of different holidays celebrated in students' native countries.

3. Show the students a picture of a traditional Thanksgiving dinner. Talk about the different foods eaten on Thanksgiving Day. Explain that the food eaten at the first Thanksgiving was probably turkey, squash, and corn.

4. Bring in magazines with pictures of food. Have students cut out pictures of what they have had or would like to have for Thanksgiving dinner. This can be done in small groups, pairs, or individually.

5. If possible, choose certain dishes to make and have your own Thanksgiving dinner in the classroom.

CHAPTER 8

Literacy Level
Page 18

1. Ask the students to mark on their calendars, or on the class calendar, the dates of independence days in their native countries.

2. Bring in magazines with pictures of food. Pass them out to small groups of students. Have them cut out the different foods they would like to take on a picnic.

3. Bring in enough poster board for each group. Have the students attach the pictures of the foods they chose. For each group, write the names of the foods they chose on a sheet of paper. With your help, have the students copy these names underneath the corresponding pictures.

4. If possible, take your students on a picnic. Have everyone share the responsibility for bringing the necessary items.

Beginning Level
Page 19

1. Bring in different paraphernalia that might be used at a Fourth of July celebration: a small American flag, sparklers, a picnic basket, etc.

2. Explain what each of these things symbolizes:

   American flag—the fifty states
      and the thirteen colonies
   sparklers and fireworks—the
      gunpowder and cannon fire of
      the revolution
   picnic basket—a picnic, a holiday

3. Design a scenario of the American Revolution so students can understand the principal ideas involved. Write the names of the original thirteen colonies on individual cards (Connecticut, Delaware, Georgia, Maryland, Massachusetts, New Hampshire, New Jersey, New York, North Carolina, Pennsylvania, Rhode Island, South Carolina, and Virginia). Show the students these states on the map to give them an idea of where events took place.

   Pass out the cards to thirteen students. Also, pass out a card with *King George III* written on it to another student. Have the student representing King George III come to the front of the class. Have someone at the front of the class hold a banner that reads *England*. Tell the class that they are part of England and King George III is the leader. Write *England* on the board.

   Now have the students representing the colonies separate themselves from the rest of the class. Give the students in the colony group a card with *Declaration of Independence, 1776* written on it. Have the student representing King George III sit down.

   Now write *1783* on the board. Give the colony group a banner that reads *United States of America*.

CHAPTER 9

Literacy Level
Page 20

1. Show students each type of coin: penny, nickel, dime, quarter, and half-dollar (if available). Write the value of each coin on the board.

2. Have students take out their change. Have them identify each coin by name and value *(penny—1¢)*.

3. Have students count their change.

4. Take the students on a tour of the school or surrounding area. Show them how to use a pay phone and a vending machine. Tell them, *"Some machines must have exact change."*

   In the classroom, help students count exact change for different amounts that you assign.

Beginning Level
Page 21

1. The following is a **timeline** activity. See page 66 for a description of timelines. Do a personal timeline for yourself: birth date, date you began (or finished) school, date you started teaching, and date of marriage (if applicable).

2. Have students do a personal timeline. Suggested dates are: birth date, date of arrival to the U.S., date they started school in the U.S., and date of marriage (if applicable).

3. The following activity is a **lineup**. See page 67 for a description of lineups. On individual cards, write: *Declaration of Independence, Christopher Columbus, George Washington,* and *Thanksgiving.* Pass out the cards to individual students. Then have them come to the front of the class with their cards. Have the other students put them in chronological order (from left to right) by telling them (in English) where to stand.

4. Circle the third Monday in February on a calendar. Explain that this is the holiday called Presidents' Day. Two important presidents, George Washington and Abraham Lincoln, are honored on this day.

CHAPTER 10

Literacy Level
Page 22

1. The following activity is a **lineup**. See page 67 for a description of lineups. Using Appendix 6 on page 52 of the student text, write the names of U.S. presidents on individual cards, at least up through Lincoln. If you feel it is appropriate, assign each student a president and have them copy the name onto the card.

2. Have each student hold up his card, one at a time. Read the name on the card out loud at least twice. Then tell the students that the people on the cards were all U.S. presidents.

3. Now read the presidents' names in order. When a name is called, have the student with the corresponding card come up to the front of the class. Have the students line up in order.

4. Be sure to ask, *"Who are the first, third, and sixteenth presidents?"* This activity also lends itself to a reinforcement of ordinal numbers (listed in Appendix 2, page 47, of the student text).

Beginning Level
Page 23

1. Write the names of the Union and Confederate states on individual cards. Pass out one card to each student (if possible). Have one card labeled *Abraham Lincoln*, and give it to another student.

2. Have the students who are holding state cards gather into one large group at the front of the class. Tell them, *"You are the United States in 1860."* Write *United States* and *1860* on the board.

3. Then have the students separate into two groups: one group of Northern states and one group of Southern states. Do not let the students refer to the map in their books until they have attempted to group themselves unassisted.

4. Tell the Northern states, *"You are the North."* Have the student representing Lincoln stand with that group. Tell the Southern states, *"You are the South."* Now tell students, *"This is what happened during the Civil War."* Write *Civil War* and *1861–1865* on the board.

5. Now have the student representing Lincoln bring the two groups together. Tell them, *"The Civil War was over. Lincoln brought the U.S. together again as one country."*

CHAPTER 11

Literacy Level
Page 24

1. Show the students the picture of Arlington National Cemetery at the top of page 24 of their texts. Write the word *cemetery* on the board. Help students make the connection between the word and the picture.

2. Show the students the pictures of soldiers on pages 24 and 25 of their texts. Tell students that soldiers are buried in Arlington National Cemetery.

    Ask the students: *"Are soldiers buried in a special place in your native country? Is there a holiday (a memorial day) in your native country to honor people killed in wars? How do you honor (remember) these people?"*

3. Using the pictures on page 24 of the student text, tell the students that Americans often put flags and flowers on soldiers' graves on Memorial Day.

4. Bring in pictures of other memorials for soldiers. Have the students draw a memorial (sign or picture) to honor loved ones, those who fought for their native country, a dead political figure they admired, or the soldiers of any country.

Beginning Level
Page 25

1. If possible, bring in pictures depicting each of the four wars discussed in this chapter. Have the students close their books. Show a picture of World War I. Write *World War I* at the top of the board. Ask the students for the years that it started and ended.

2. Using a timeline, give a brief history of each war. A world map or globe would be helpful for this presentation.

World War I: 1914–1918; between the Allies (Great Britain, France, the Soviet Union, Italy, and the U.S.) and the Central Powers (Germany, Austria-Hungary, Turkey, etc.).

World War II: 1939–1945; between the Allies (Great Britain, France, the Soviet Union, and the U.S.) and the Axis (Germany, Italy, and Japan).

Korean War: 1950–1953; North Korea and China against South Korea and the United Nations (including the U.S. and excluding the Soviet Union).

Vietnam War: 1954–1972; North Vietnam against South Vietnam and the U.S. Explain that many Americans had different opinions about American involvement in the war.

3. The following is a **chart** activity. See page 66 for a description of charts. List the major countries involved in the war on one side of the board. Then make a two-columned chart on the board. Label one column *Allies* and the other column *Central Powers.* Beginning with the United States, have the students choose which column each country belongs in.

4. Get copies of a world map that can be colored in, one for each student. Bring colored pens, markers, or crayons. Start with World War I. Have students label their maps according to the war they are working with. Using the two-columned chart on the board, have the students color the Allies one color and the Central Powers another color. Keep students' maps so they can compare them after they have completed all four wars.

5. Repeat 1–4 with each war discussed in this chapter. Remember to show a picture of each war before beginning the board activity.

6. Show the picture of a factory on page 28. Tell the students that since so many men fought in World War I and World War II, women had to work in all of the factories. Tell the students that in the next chapter they will learn about different kinds of jobs.

CHAPTER 12
Literacy Level
Page 26

1. Bring in pictures of different workers from magazines and newspapers. First, show the pictures one at a time, and discuss what each one is. Then write the corresponding words for the pictures on the board. Say each word aloud.

2. Go back through the pictures. Hold up a picture in front of the class. Ask, *"Who is this?"* Then have a student come up and point to the corresponding word on the board. This activity may also be done with pictures of different workplaces or uniforms.

3. The following activity is a **matchup**. See page 66 for a description of matchups. If possible, have different pictures of workers, their workplaces, and/or their uniforms. Have the students work in pairs or small groups to match up the pictures.

4. Have the students tell (and/or show) the jobs they had in their native countries. Use the pictures from activities 1 and 3 to aid students.

5. Have the students tell (and/or show) the jobs they have in the United States. After completing this activity, have the students choose jobs they would like to have from the pictures. Another alternative is to have the students draw pictures of jobs they have had or would like to have.

6. Have individual students act out what their jobs are. Have the rest of the class guess the job. Write each job on the board. You may also have students act out the jobs they would like to have.

Beginning Level
Page 27

1. Bring magazine and newspaper pictures similar to the ones used in numbers 1 and 2 from the literacy level activities above. Discuss each picture before you begin the activity. Write labels for the pictures on strips of paper or on index cards. Hand out a picture or label to each student. Have them try to find the matching picture or label by asking questions, for example: *"Is he in a restaurant? Does he work with food? Does he cook?"*

2. To illustrate dangerous situations, use examples from household products first. Bring in containers with warning labels on them and be sure to make it clear to students why these things can be dangerous. Make a special effort in pointing out the labels.

3. Show students other warning signs and symbols. These can range from road signs to workplace warnings.

4. If possible, find different illustrations of dangerous workplace situations. Explain to students if any of the situations are against the law.

5. Have students stage different dangerous workplace situations. Have students come up to the staged dangerous workplace, and have them make it into a safe workplace.

6. Find out if any students are union members. If some are members, have them name some good things (benefits) their unions have helped them with. Also, find out if students can name some bad things about their unions. List both the good and bad points on the board.

   Now have nonunion students name some good things (benefits) their jobs (or companies) offer. Then have them name some bad things about their jobs. List both on the board. Now compare the union and nonunion lists. Ask students, *"Which one do you like best?"*

7. Bring in some pictures with headlines or captions about strikes. Ask the students: *"What does this picture show? What are these people doing? Does it have to do with work?"*

   Explain to the students that workers (teachers, pilots, truck drivers, etc.) strike because they want better things from their jobs.

☙

CHAPTER 13
Literacy Level
Page 28

1. The following is a **chart** activity. See page 66 for a description of chart activities. Make three separate charts about the good and bad points of the students' schools, workplaces, and homes. Find out some of the things that students would like changed.

2. Bring poster board and markers to make protest signs. Use ideas from the charts on things that students would like changed. Make sure students are given the words they need to make the signs.

3. Have the students act out the things that are wrong with their homes or neighborhoods, for example, apartment rules not allowing children. Also have them act out problems or things they do not like at work, for example, unequal pay for similar jobs or no promotions.

Beginning Level
Page 29

1. Continue the slogan exercise from page 29 of the student text. Write the categories on the board. List the following slogans on one side of the board: *Heat Our Homes! Build New Schools! Elect Gloria Chen! Equal Pay for Equal Work!* Have the students tell you where to write which slogan.

2. Have students develop their own slogans from things that are important and needed by them.

   Make a list of these new slogans on the board next to the categories. Again, have students place them under the correct heading.

3. Talk about civil rights. Ask students if they think we now have equal education, housing, voting, and jobs (equal pay for equal work).

☙

CHAPTER 14

Literacy Level
Page 32

1. Mount pictures of the president, your governor, and your mayor (if applicable) on poster board. Have the students answer personal identification questions about each person. Ask the students: *"What is his first name? What is his last name? What is his job? In what city does he work?"*

2. Ask students about the leaders in their native countries. These can range from local and religious leaders to national leaders. Discuss with students what makes a good leader. Find out if students think each leader is good or bad. Allow room for differing opinions. Be sure to include U.S. and foreign leaders in this discussion.

3. The following is a **chart** activity. See page 66 for a description of chart activities. Draw a two-columned chart on the board. Label one column *Good Leaders* and the other column *Bad Leaders*. Have students put the leaders discussed in number 2 in their respective columns. Write their choices on the board.

Beginning Level
Page 33

The following activity is a **matchup**. See page 66 for a description of matchups. Design a matchup activity of important people, positions, and places. On individual 3x5-inch index cards, write *president*, *vice president*, *governor*, and *mayor*. On separate cards, write the officeholder's name, what building he works in, and the city and state he works in. An example appears at the bottom of this page.

CHAPTER 15

Literacy Level
Page 34

1. To help students understand taxes better, bring in a few sales receipts. Circle the sales tax on each, and pass the receipts around the classroom. Then write some examples on the board. Demonstrate for students the subtotal, the sales tax, and the final total. Then have students identify each of the above on other examples.

    Using the pictures on page 34 of the student text and your surroundings, indicate that taxes are used to pay for schools and roads.

2. Bring in a book containing pictures of road signs. If possible, make copies of the signs for each student. Discuss the signs you feel students should be familiar with. Be sure students understand that these laws are for safety purposes.

3. Write the word *immunization* on the board and indicate the appropriate picture on page 34 of the student text. Then list some of the diseases that children are inoculated against: measles, diphtheria, tetanus, etc.

Beginning Level
Page 35

1. The literacy level activities above are also appropriate for this level. A discussion of road signs will prove useful for numbers 2 and 3 below. Be sure to ask students if and where they have seen such signs.

2. Explain to students that laws can be changed. Use speed limits as one example. Write two speed limits on the board. Raise one speed limit and lower the other. Examples of new stop signs or streets changing from two-way to one-way can also be used.

    If you did the exercise involving sales receipts, tell students that sales taxes can also be changed (usually raised).

| president | Bill Clinton | White House | Washington, D.C. |
| governor | Jim Edgar | state capitol building | Springfield, IL |

3. Have the students observe the signs around their school and homes. Have them draw pictures of changes they would like to see regarding the signs you have discussed.

CHAPTER 16
Literacy Level
Page 36

1. Discuss the U.S. laws regarding permanent residency. Refer to pages 68–73 of this guide for more information.

2. Talk about marriage laws, such as required blood tests and marriage licenses.

    Ask students, *"Who is married?"* Ask those students who are married, *"Where were you married?"* Find out if there were special marriage laws where students got married.

    Explain the term *engaged* to students. Ask students, *"Is anyone engaged?"* If so, find out when they are to be married.

3. Discuss different local laws with students such as pedestrian right-of-way, school-zone speed limits, parking permits, and drinking ages.

Beginning Level
Page 37

1. The following is a **chart** activity. See page 66 for a description of chart activities. Draw a chart of local laws (or rules) starting at a level where students will have had direct experience. Have the students give you ideas to choose from. For example, begin with your classroom: *Class begins at _____, class ends at _____, break time begins at _____ and ends at _____, no children in the classroom,* etc.

    Then move on to your school building: *All cars must have parking stickers, no smoking in the halls, smoking permitted in the lounge, no food or drink in the halls,* etc.

    Do the same for students' workplaces, homes, neighborhoods, and city or town.

    Ask the students, *"Who enforces these laws (rules)? What happens if these laws (rules) are broken?"* Do so for each level of the chart.

2. Bring in pictures of the students' local and state representatives (either from a newspaper or the representatives' local offices). Have the students learn who their representatives are.

CHAPTER 17
Literacy Level
Page 38

1. Set up mock trials. Choose students to be the lawyers, judge, jury, witnesses, and defendant. Create different situations to be tried. For example, if a student came in late, make him the defendant. Select students for the jury and choose students who were on time as witnesses. Tell the lawyers (students) what to say. Have the prosecuting lawyer tell the defendant what he is accused of. Then have both lawyers ask witnesses, in turn, what they saw.

2. After all of the evidence has been presented, have the jury talk over and decide guilty or not guilty. Have the judge make the announcement. Be sure to keep this activity lighthearted and in the spirit of fun and learning.

Beginning Level
Page 39

1. Expand on the Listen and Answer activity on page 39 of the student text. Discuss situations you feel your students should know about. For example, Victor's car is weaving from side to side on the road. The police pull Victor over. Victor has been drinking alcohol. Is Victor breaking the law? What might happen?

    Having students act out different scenarios may help students to understand the different situations.

2. Talk about people's rights if they are arrested. Define by illustration or example: the right to an attorney (lawyer); if you can't pay for one, one is provided for (given to) you; you don't have to say anything, especially against yourself, etc.

CHAPTER 18

Literacy Level
Page 40

Using the issues given at the bottom of page 40 of the student text, have students vote on the issue of guns/no guns. Provide uniform pieces of paper for each student. If possible, have *yes* and *no* written on each piece of paper. Students can then circle their choice. If it isn't possible, students may write their choice (*yes* or *no*). Collect the ballots, count them, and write the results on the board. Do the same for the second issue.

For the third issue, break it into two separate issues. First have them vote *yes* or *no* on Dukakis and then on Bush. (If this is too dated, use a current set of candidates.)

Make sure students do not put their names on the ballots. Make sure they know that everybody's vote in the U.S. is secret.

Beginning Level
Page 41

1. Take your class through the changes in voting laws.

    Begin by writing *1789* on the board. Ask the students: *"Who in this class could have voted in 1789?"* Give explanations to their responses. Don't forget to include yourself.

    Repeat this procedure for each year presented on the timeline.

    Now ask, *"Who could vote today?"* If students haven't raised this issue already, introduce the topic of citizenship. Explain to them that only U.S. citizens can vote in U.S. elections.

2. Bring in a picture of a white man, white woman, black woman, black man, Hispanic woman, Hispanic man, etc. Show each picture to the class and ask, *"Could he/she have voted in 1789?"* Repeat the question using different years.

CHAPTER 19

Literacy Level
Page 42

1. Make a copy of the American flag for each student. Have the students count the total number of stripes (thirteen). Then ask them, *"How many dark stripes are there?"* Indicate the number of dark stripes (seven). Ask the students, *"What color are these stripes on an American flag?"* (Red.) Use an example to make sure students know what color red is and how to spell it.

    Repeat this with the remaining stripes. Then ask the students: *"How many stars are there?"* (Fifty.) *"What color are they?"* (White.) Now indicate the background of the stars. Ask the students, *"What color is this?"* (Blue.) Use an example to make sure students know what color blue is and how to spell it.

2. Bring in colored pencils or markers. Have the students draw and color flags.

3. Bring in a recording of the "Star-Spangled Banner." Tell students, *"This is our national anthem (song). It is talking about the American flag."*

    Refer students to Appendix 7 on page 53 of their texts. Have them follow along as you play the recording.

4. Repeat number 3 with the Pledge of Allegiance. If a recording is not available, read it out loud once, and then have students repeat each phrase after you. Explain that the Pledge of Allegiance is said facing the flag with the right hand over the heart. The Pledge expresses respect for the flag and the United States.

Beginning Level
Page 43

1. Have the students work with copies of the American flag. As a review, have them count the dark stripes. Ask them: *"How many are there? What color are they?"*

2. a. Have the students construct their own American flags. First review the different parts of the flag with students. Remind them that there are thirteen stripes: seven red and six white. Also, there are fifty white stars on a blue background.

b. Bring in large sheets of paper or white poster board. If this is not possible, use typing or copying paper. Also bring in your choice of colored pencils, markers, or construction paper (in the appropriate colors). Have other colors available so that students will have to choose the correct colors. If you decide to use construction paper, you will also need scissors and glue or tape.

c. Have students work in small groups to assemble their own American flags.

3. a. Display the flags around the classroom. Assign a number to each flag. Then hold a secret ballot to choose the best flag. Have the students write the number of the flag that they think is best. Count the votes, display the three largest totals, and announce a winner.

b. Give a first-place ribbon for the winning flag. (If you want, give homemade or token prizes for the members of the group.) Also, second- or third-place ribbons can help demonstrate ordinal numbers (listed on page 47 of the student text).

c. As an alternative, have students construct the flags of their native countries.

4. Bring in pictures of other symbols. Label them with the city and state where they can be found. Have the students post them on a large wall map of the United States.

CHAPTER 20
Literacy Level
Page 44

1. The following is a **chart** activity. See page 66 for a description of chart activities. Make a chart like the one at the bottom of the page to compare the rights of a permanent resident with those of a citizen.

    Have the students tell you *yes* or *no* for each category, beginning with permanent resident. Make sure students understand how the chart works before beginning the activity. Do an example for them.

2. Have the students draw pictures of the rights of a permanent resident and a naturalized citizen. Use Katrina and Jan from page 44 of the student text as examples. Students could draw pictures of a house (or apartment), a work setting (or uniform), figures representing a family, and a ballot.

Beginning Level
Page 45

1. The following is a **sequencing** activity. See page 67 for a description of sequencing. Break down the Pledge of Allegiance into the following phrases:

    I pledge allegiance to the flag
    of the United States of America
    and to the Republic for which it
    *   stands,*
    one nation under God,
    *   indivisible,*
    with liberty and justice for all.

	United States			
	Live	Work	Vote	Family
Permanent Resident				
Citizen				

Write these phrases on strips of paper. Divide the class into small groups. Give each group a complete set of strips. Have the students put the Pledge in order.

2. Write out the practice questions from page 45 of the student text on strips of paper, then put all the strips in a box. Have a student pull out a question, and ask him or another student that question.

3. The following activity is a **lineup**. See page 67 for a description of lineups. Give four students a card with one of the following names written on it: George Washington, Abraham Lincoln, Ronald Reagan, and Bill Clinton. Have the students come up to the front of the class and arrange themselves in order of who became president first.

   You can adapt this activity to cover the other people studied in the student text, for example, American Indians, Christopher Columbus, Pilgrims, George Washington, Abraham Lincoln, and Martin Luther King, Jr.

APPENDIX 8
Pages 54-55

1. Go over the alphabet with students. Have them repeat each letter after you. You may need to do this a few times.

2. Have students practice saying and spelling their names and addresses. Have them practice writing their names and addresses. Be sure to have them capitalize the correct letters.

3. Take students for a walk around the school and/or classroom. Have students name things that they recognize. Provide the words for those things that they do not know the names of. Build up their vocabulary. Repeat the tour at a later date.

4. Choose a word to have students spell. Indicate the number of letters in the word by writing the corresponding number of blanks on the board. Have one student at a time guess a letter. If he guesses a wrong letter, write that letter on the board to the side. If he guesses a correct letter, write it in the correct blank. Continue in this fashion until someone guesses the word. This helps students learn the English alphabet and helps them learn how to spell different words. Point out to students which words need to be capitalized.

Special Activity Types

The following activity types appear in the preceding extension activities.

CHARTS AND TIMELINES

The purpose of using charts and timelines is to provide a basis for conversation and/or writing activities.

Format: Always provide a reference chart or timeline on the board for students to refer to. Provide examples and be sure students know what is being asked of them. Have students discuss their answers before completing the activity.

INFORMATION GAPS

The purpose of an information gap is to provide the groundwork for conversation and information gathering.

Format: An information gap is a paired activity in which one student has half of the information, and the other student has the other half. The students must work together, communicating in English, to complete the assignment given to them.

You can make the exercise easier by taking the role of Student A yourself and having the rest of the class take the role of Student B. This way the students can see the exercise modeled and understand how they are to find the missing information they need.

After you feel confident that students can handle the exercise on their own, pair up students and ask them to complete the information gaps in pairs.

MATCHUPS

The purpose of a matchup is to reinforce vocabulary, check comprehension, and get students actively involved.

Format: Write the words or phrases on individual cards. Pass out cards at random to the students. Have them find the card that matches their own by asking other students questions in English about their cards. This activity can be done in a large group, small groups, or pairs.

Variations

1. To play a concentration game, put all of the cards face down on a table. Have one

student at a time turn over two cards. If the cards are a match, the student gets to keep the pair and try again. If they do not match, turn the cards back over and have another student try to find a match. The student with the most matched pairs wins.

2. For beginning level students, vocabulary words and corresponding pictures may be used.

3. Category cards may also be used. For example, city, state, and country can be used as categories. Students must match cards naming the different cities, states, and countries with the correct categories.

SEQUENCING

The purpose of sequencing is to actively involve students in comprehension checks.

Format: Provide students with information that needs to be placed in order. Have students work in small groups, pairs, or individually, depending on the activity and class size. Students are then asked to put the items in a specific order.

LINEUPS

The purpose of a lineup is to actively involve students in the learning process.

Format: A lineup requires students to physically line up in a particular order. The order of the line depends on the nature of the activity. An example of a lineup is to have the students line up in alphabetical order according to their first names. This gives the students a chance to practice asking each other their names. Students may also need to ask how to spell a name and then have to listen to the response. This also helps the students practice putting things in alphabetical order.

STORY RETELLING

The purpose of story retelling is to check listening and/or reading comprehension.

Format: Read the story to the students two or three times. Have the students retell the story in their own words to reinforce and further understand the story.

What Is the Amnesty Program?

What is popularly referred to as "The Amnesty Program" is the result of federal legislation: the Immigration Reform and Control Act of 1986 (IRCA). This legislation seeks to improve control over immigration into the United States and to address the reality of the presence of millions of undocumented residents in this country.

To improve attempts to limit illegal immigration, IRCA mandates that certain undocumented residents living in the United States be given the opportunity to attain legal status. Amnesty was offered to persons who could prove that they had resided here continuously since January 1, 1982. (Undocumented workers who did not live in the United States before January 1982 could apply for amnesty if they were employed in agriculture; these people are referred to as Special Agricultural Workers [SAWs].)

FIRST STEP

To begin the process of becoming a legal resident, an undocumented person was required to apply for temporary residency during the period from May 5, 1987, to May 4, 1988. (SAWs could apply for temporary residency as late as November 30, 1988.) This initiated what is referred to as the **first step** in the amnesty program. In the first step, a person submitted an application to the Immigration and Naturalization Service (INS)

that demonstrated, through the use of receipts, proof of bank accounts, etc., that he or she had indeed resided in the United States since January 1, 1982.

Upon receiving temporary residency, the applicant was given a temporary residence card which entitled him or her to live in the United States for a period of thirty months from the date of application.

SECOND STEP

Beginning on the date that a person applied for temporary residency, he or she is required to wait eighteen months before applying for permanent residency. The **second step** begins after this eighteen-month waiting period. During the second step, the individual has a period of exactly one year to apply for permanent residency.

It is important to understand that in the second step an individual must apply for permanent residency. Failure to make this adjustment from temporary to permanent residency will cause the temporary resident to revert back to illegal status. (Note that SAWs do not need to apply for permanent residency, but will automatically be adjusted to permanent status after eighteen months of temporary residency.)

During the period of temporary residency, the individual must abide by certain restrictions. He or she may not leave the United

States for more than a total of ninety days, and any single absence from the U.S. may not be longer than thirty days. (SAWs have more lenient travel restrictions.) Also, the applicant will be denied permanent residency if he or she commits a felony or more than two misdemeanors as a temporary resident. Furthermore, the applicant may not receive certain types of public assistance benefits as a temporary resident.

Educational Requirements

The applicant for permanent residency must satisfy another important requirement. Upon submission of the application for permanent residency, the applicant must prove that he or she has a knowledge of the English language and American civics. (Note: the English/civics requirement does not apply to SAWs.)

There are several ways that temporary residents can satisfy the English/civics requirement. The applicant can:

- Take an oral and written examination at an INS office

- Demonstrate that he or she has taken at least forty hours of English/civics classes at an INS-approved institution

- Demonstrate that he or she has attended a certified school in the U.S. as a full-time student for one year, and that the year of school included forty hours of instruction in English and civics

- Produce evidence of having passed the GED. If the Spanish GED was taken, it must have included the section that tests knowledge of English.

- Pass a standardized test that will be offered at approved institutions

Many persons applying for amnesty will choose to take a forty-hour course in order to satisfy the English/civics requirement. The applicant who successfully completes this course will receive a "Certificate of Satisfactory Pursuit" from the approved institution. The presentation of this certificate to the INS will absolve the applicant from having to take any sort of test with the INS.

Many institutions that provide English/civics courses will receive federal reimbursement for some of their expenditures. This federal funding is part of a program

referred to as State Legalization Impact Assistance Grants (SLIAG). SLIAG funds were mandated by the IRCA legislation, and their purpose is to assist states in implementing the amnesty program. The method of distribution of SLIAG funds varies from state to state.

PERMANENT RESIDENCY

Persons who successfully complete steps one and two of the amnesty program will receive permanent residency in the United States. Note, however, that a "permanent resident" does not have precisely the same status as a "citizen" of the United States.

A permanent resident in the United States has the right to indefinitely work and live in this country. However, a permanent resident does not have the right to vote, nor will he or she receive the full benefit of certain government programs such as social security. Also, it is easier for citizens of the United States to apply to have nonresident family members be admitted to the United States as permanent residents.

A permanent resident may apply to become a citizen of the United States after he or she has been a permanent resident for five years. To become a citizen, a permanent resident must demonstrate a knowledge of the English language and U.S. civics in a test at the INS. It should be pointed out that individuals in English/civics classes of the amnesty program are potentially receiving valuable preparation for the test necessary to become a citizen of the United States. Note that the INS test for citizenship may be taken at the interview which occurs when a person receives permanent residency. The individual who takes this test when becoming a permanent resident will not need to repeat it when applying for citizenship five years later.

The following student handout, in English and Spanish, gives basic information on the steps to permanent residency. Please feel free to duplicate and hand out this information to your students.

Robert M. Paral
Research Associate
National Association
of Latino Elected
and Appointed Officials
(NALEO)

How to Become a Permanent Resident Through the Amnesty Program

What is the amnesty program?

For persons who lived in the United States without proper documentation, the amnesty program offers an opportunity to become a permanent, legal resident of this country.

The amnesty program has two important steps:

During the period from May 5, 1987, to May 4, 1988, an undocumented resident could apply for temporary residency in the United States. After applying for temporary residency, the applicant has to wait eighteen months before applying for permanent residency. The eighteen months of temporary residency are the **first step** of the amnesty program.

The **second step** of the amnesty program begins after a person has completed eighteen months of temporary residency. The applicant then has exactly one year in which to apply for permanent residency. A temporary resident who fails to apply for permanent residency will revert back to illegal status. (Note that persons employed in agriculture do not need to apply for permanent residency; they will receive permanent residency automatically after completing eighteen months of temporary residency. Persons employed in agriculture could also apply for temporary residency as late as November 30, 1988.)

How does a person apply for permanent residency?

To complete the second step, it is necessary to submit an application to the Immigration and Naturalization Service. Persons who have temporary residency will receive this application in the mail toward the end of the eighteen months of temporary residency.

What are other requirements to complete the second step?

In order to receive permanent residency, many—although not all—applicants will have to demonstrate an understanding of the English language and the United States government. There are several options for complying with this requirement. These options include:

• taking a class on the English language and the United States government. Upon completing this class, the student will receive a certificate that verifies that he or she has an understanding of these subjects.

• OR, taking an oral and written test at the Immigration and Naturalization Service

• OR, giving proof of having attended an accredited school in the U.S. full-time for a period of one year, during which the student received at least forty hours of instruction in English and United States civics

- OR, giving proof of having passed the GED exam. The Spanish GED exam will be accepted only if the individual also took the English-language section of the GED.

- OR, passing an INS-approved test at certain schools and community centers throughout the United States

Apart from complying with the English/civics requirement, it is important that temporary residents do not leave the United States for a total of more than ninety days, and that no single absence from the United States last more than thirty days. (Note that there are certain other restrictions that temporary residents must adhere to.)

What requirements are there for persons who work in agriculture?

Persons who work in agriculture (and who have a temporary resident card numbered 210A) do not have to satisfy an English/civics requirement. These persons may also leave the United States an unlimited number of times, as long as no single absence from the United States lasts more than six months.

How can I get more information about the amnesty program?

For information in English or Spanish about the amnesty program, call NALEO, the National Association of Latino Elected and Appointed Officials, at 1-800-44-NALEO (in California, call 1-800-34-NALEO). There is no charge for the phone call.

Cómo Hacerse Residente Permanente Dentro del Programa de Amnistía

¿Qué es el programa de amnistía?

Para gente que ha vivido en los Estados Unidos sin documentación legal, el programa de amnistía ofrece una oportunidad de hacerse residente permanente y legal de este país.

El programa de amnistía consiste de dos pasos:

En el período entre el cinco de mayo de 1987 y el cuatro de mayo de 1988, se podía solicitar la residencia temporal en los Estados Unidos. Después de solicitar la residencia temporal, el solicitante tiene que esperar dieciocho meses antes de solicitar la residencia permanente. Los dieciocho meses de residencia temporal se llaman **el primer paso** del programa de amnistía.

El segundo paso del programa de amnistía empieza al cumplir dieciocho meses de residencia temporal. Al acabar los dieciocho meses, empieza un período de **un año** en que es obligatorio solicitar la residencia permanente. Si un residente temporal no solicita la residencia permanente, volverá a ser indocumentado en este país. (Nótese que personas que trabajan en la agricultura no necesitan solicitar la residencia permanente; ésta la recibirán automáticamente al cumplir el período de residencia temporal. Personas que trabajan en la agricultura tenían hasta el 30 de noviembre de 1988 para solicitar la residencia temporal.)

¿Cómo se solicita la residencia permanente?

Para cumplir con el segundo paso hay que entregar una solicitud al Servicio de Inmigración y Naturalización. Las personas que tienen residencia temporal recibirán esta solicitud por correo hacia el final de los dieciocho meses de residencia temporal.

¿Qué otros requisitos hay para cumplir con el segundo paso?

Antes de recibir residencia permanente, muchos—aunque no todos—de los solicitantes tendrán que demostrar que tienen un conocimiento del inglés y de cómo funciona el gobierno estadounidense. Se puede cumplir con este requisito de varias maneras. Se puede:

• tomar un curso sobre el inglés y el gobierno estadounidense. Al acabar con este curso, el/la estudiante recibirá un certificado que verifica que el/ella tiene un conocimiento del inglés y del gobierno estadounidense.

• o, ir al Servicio de Inmigración y Naturalización y tomar un examen que tiene partes orales y partes escritas.

• o, mostrar prueba de haber asistido tiempo completo durante un año, a una escuela autorizada en este país, donde el alumno recibió cuarenta horas de instrucción sobre inglés y gobierno.

- o, mostrar prueba de haber aprobado el examen de **GED** (el diploma de equivalencia de la escuela secundaria). Se aceptará el **GED** en español sólo si la persona también tomó la parte del examen que trata del inglés.

- o, tomar un examen aprobado por el Servicio de Inmigración y Naturalización que será ofrecido en ciertas escuelas y centros comunitarios en los Estados Unidos.

Además de demostrar un concocimiento del inglés y del gobierno estadounidense, es preciso que una persona con residencia temporal no salga de los Estados Unidos por un total de más de noventa dias, y que no haga ningun viaje fuera del país que dure más de treinta dias a la vez. (Nótese que existen ciertos otros requisitos para recibir residencia permanente.)

¿Qué requisitos hay para personas que trabajan en la agricultura?

Personas que trabajan en la agricultura (y que tienen tarjeta de residencia temporal que lleva el numero 210A) no necesitan demostrar ningun concocimiento del inglés ni del gobierno estadounidense. Además, estas personas pueden salir del país por un numero ilimitado de veces; sólo que ninguna salida dure más de seis meses.

¿Cómo puedo conseguir más información sobre el programa de amnistía?

Para informacíon en español e inglés sobre la amnistía, llame a NALEO, la Asociación Nacional de Funcionarios Latinos Electos y Designados, al 1-800-44-NALEO (en California, llame al 1-800-34-NALEO). La llamada es gratis.

About the Contributors to This Series

Carole Cross coordinates the ESL program of El Monte-Rosemead Adult School in El Monte, California. In her capacity as coordinator, she has worked to develop minilessons for students fulfilling the educational requirement of the amnesty program. Ms. Cross has taught American history and English for sixteen years, and she holds a Ph.D. in education.

Rob Paral is a research associate at NALEO (National Association of Latino Elected and Appointed Officials) in Washington, D.C. A former ESL teacher, Mr. Paral has been a contributing writer for language textbooks and an editor of educational materials. He holds an M.A. in Spanish.

Betsy Rubin has been teaching English as a second language for more than a decade. She has taught students of all educational backgrounds and at all levels of language ability. Ms. Rubin has also served as an editorial consultant for educational materials and is the author of Contemporary's six-book *Edge on English* series. She holds an M.A. in TESL.

Ann Van Slyke has had a wide variety of experience in teaching English as a second language to adults. She has also served as a statewide ESL consultant at the Illinois ESL Adult Education Service Center. Ms. Van Slyke has had extensive experience in teacher training, including working as a Fulbright lecturer in TEFL, and holds an M.A. in TESL.

Sally Wigginton is ESL/Methods Instructor and Supervisor of Student Teaching at the Urban Education Program/Associated Colleges of the Midwest in Chicago, Illinois. She has taught English as a second language to adults for twelve years. Ms. Wigginton has an M.A. in linguistics/TESL and is pursuing an M.A. in reading.

Give Your Amnesty/ESL Students a

LOOK AT THE U·S·

* Based on the content of the federal citizenship texts
* Designed to meet INS amnesty instructional requirements
* Content-based materials that promote listening, speaking, reading, and writing skills
* Special pictorial-based literacy book aimed at literacy level and beginning level students
* Can be used in amnesty and ESL classrooms and for citizenship preparation

An Innovative, Multi-Level Program

With a focus on developing and reinforcing the skills of listening, speaking, reading, and writing, this multi-level series enables you to manage a continuum of students with English abilities ranging from literacy to advanced. Thus, civics concepts can be taught at the appropriate level of English instruction.

Literacy Level Text

The literacy level text provides basic material for both *literacy level* and *beginning level* students. Consistent thematic content throughout this text's 20 lessons is first presented in a pictorial-based format. The short, easy-to-follow reading in each lesson gives beginning level students the additional opportunity to work with brief written text and activities.

Book 1 and Book 2

Each student text addresses the same key concepts in U.S. history and government. However, since students have varying degrees of proficiency in English, the books are written at different levels. The 21 consistently designed lessons incorporate activities that promote English-language acquisition through a content-based approach.

Contemporary Books, a division of
NTC/Contemporary Publishing Company,
4255 West Touhy Avenue, Lincolnwood
(Chicago), Illinois, 60646-1975, U.S.A.
(800) 621-1918

ORDER FORM
April 1, 1989

BILL TO _____

NAME _____

ADDRESS _____

CITY, STATE, ZIP _____

PURCHASE ORDER NO. _____

DATE _____

SHIP TO _____

NAME _____

ADDRESS _____

CITY, STATE, ZIP _____

BUYER _____

PHONE NO. _____

QUANTITY	TITLE NO.	TITLE	NET PRICE
	4329-6	LOOK AT THE U.S.—LITERACY LEVEL	$11.00
	4328-8	TEACHER'S GUIDE—LITERACY LEVEL	8.75
	4387-3	LOOK AT THE U.S.—BOOK 1	11.00
	4386-5	LOOK AT THE U.S.—BOOK 2	11.00
	4380-6	TEACHER'S GUIDE—BOOKS 1 & 2	8.75

Net prices subject to change without notice. The net prices quoted on this order form are exclusive of freight costs, which will be prepaid and added to your invoice. The net prices represent our prices to institutional customers and are not intended to control the resale price. All terms net 30 days. F.O.B. Chicago.